Building the Resilient Community

Building the Resilient Community

Lessons from the Lost Boys of Sudan

M. JAN HOLTON

CASCADE *Books* · Eugene, Oregon

BUILDING THE RESILIENT COMMUNITY
Lessons from the Lost Boys of Sudan

Cascade Books
An Imprint of Wipf and Stock Publishers
199 W. 8th Ave., Suite 3
Eugene, OR 97401

www.wipfandstock.com

ISBN 13: 978-1-60899-245-4

Cataloging-in-Publication data:

Holton, M. Jan.

Building the resilient community : lessons from the lost boys of Sudan / M. Jan Holton.

x + 176 p.; 23 cm. Includes bibliographical references and index.

ISBN 13: 978-1-60899-245-4

1. Refugees—Sudan. 2. Christianity—Sudan. 3. Pastoral Care. I. Title.

BV4012.2 .H55 2011

Manufactured in the U.S.A.

Earlier versions of sections from chapter 5 and the introduction first appeared in the *Journal for Pastoral Theology* 20.1 (2010) and are reprinted here with permission.

Cover photo: Kakuma Refugee Camp, Kenya, © 2003 M. Jan Holton.

This book is dedicated to refugees around the world

who long for a safe place to call home.

Contents

Tables

Acknowledgments

I AM DEEPLY GRATEFUL FOR THE MANY PEOPLE WHO HAVE helped make this research possible. First and foremost I thank the Lost Boy refugees in Nashville, Tennessee, the people of the Abang community in Bor, Sudan, and the refugees in Kakuma Refugee Camp—all of whom so willingly shared their stories with me. Their immense generosity and hospitality have left a profound mark on my life. I am thankful and deeply indebted to Mading Gai Arou, Achuouth Deng Kur, and "Cousin John" in Sudan for their kindness, courage, faith, and strength that continue to inspire me.

The research in Bor, Sudan, was made possible by funding through the Lilly Theological Research Grants Program. It was further supplemented by a MacMillan Center Faculty Research Grant at Yale University. I am thankful to Yale University Divinity School for the sabbatical that allowed me to complete the writing of this book and extend my gratitude also to Vanderbilt University for support during the earliest part of this research while I was in graduate school. I am likewise grateful to Hillsboro Presbyterian Church in Nashville, Tennessee, for the many ways they have supported this research and, more important, the ways they have loved, sustained, and learned from the Lost Boys and their families.

I am indebted to the United Nations High Commissioner for Refugees (UNHCR) office in Bor, Sudan, and Kakuma for allowing me access to safe accommodations in Bor and to be one of only a few researchers allowed to visit Kakuma.

Kalbryn McLean has been an invaluable resource through the development of this manuscript, for which I am more grateful than I can ever express. And, to the many colleagues, friends, and family for your unwavering encouragement and support, I say, thank you.

Introduction

It was somewhat past midnight as I waited with a large group of volunteers in the Nashville airport for the arrival of four Lost Boy refugees. The refugees were the last to deplane, ensuring, along with the late hour, that we were nearly the only ones left in the arrival area. Finally, four very tall, thin young men with rich dark skin emerged through the door. They seemed to look both apprehensive and excited. When greeted with cheers of welcome, wide grins swept across their faces. Almost immediately the church volunteers surrounded the young men, gathered hands, and offered a prayer of thanks for their safe arrival. To be frank, I was a bit taken aback by this forceful show of religious expression and was worried that the refugees would feel overwhelmed or intimidated. In retrospect, I now understand that there could not have been a more appropriate way to welcome these devout Christian young men into our part of the world.

Three years later, it was me stepping off a plane into the heat and dust of Kakuma Refugee Camp. I carried with me what sounded like modern-day "epistles" from the very same refugees I had welcomed years before that encouraged their brothers and sisters in Christ still in Kakuma to accept me as if I were family. Prepared only as much as I could be to witness the tragedy of lives held in limbo, I stepped into their world.

IN 2000 I RECEIVED AN EXTENSION MINISTRY APPOINT-ment as United Methodist clergy to work with the Catholic Charities Refugee Resettlement Program in Nashville, Tennessee. Shortly thereafter, we became involved in resettling over sixty refugees known as the Lost Boys of Sudan. This task presented us with many challenges and many blessings, though some days we could not tell which was which. It did not take long for me to realize, however, that these were extraordinary young men. Though all pre-arrival reports stressed the traumatic circumstances surrounding these young lives, few mentioned their overwhelmingly resilient nature, which soon became quite apparent. For example, nearly all of the young men told of watching loved ones die, sometimes in horrible ways, and of having their own lives threatened over long periods of time. For years, images of these events replayed themselves through dreams or what we might call flashbacks. Yet the Lost Boys were highly adaptive to their new surroundings and ultimately were able to negotiate the very tricky transitions related to culture, faith, and the workplace. How can young men who have suffered such a tragic early life adapt to so much change and function so well in difficult circumstances? In short, why are they so resilient? These are the questions that drive me to understand the Lost Boys and their experience.

My aim in this book is to explore how the obligations of mutual care and spiritual traditions, particularly healing traditions, of the Dinka community have shaped the lives of the Lost Boys and become a resource for healing, especially under circumstances of sustained trauma. More specifically, how have the deeply instilled beliefs and traditions, especially their Christian faith, helped, or not helped, a group of young refugees not only survive the atrocities of war but learn to thrive amid such adversity? Going one step further, I propose that what we learn about the Lost Boys and the entire Dinka community can be a resource for learning in our own communities of faith in the United States. What I have discovered is a startling concept of community that reflects their sense of deeply ingrained obligation toward the other and a powerful faith narrative that empowers them to participate in God's promise of healing and redemption. This disposition lays a foundation for resilience in the face of adversity and has helped mitigate the effects of their traumatic experiences.

While there are many dimensions to this mutual care, I will focus on three significant practices that in turn contribute to a communal faith narrative. Even in times of great peril, the Lost Boys created among themselves a relatively safe holding place, articulated justice (in relative terms), and voiced a collective trauma story. These have allowed the young men to become highly functioning individuals in spite of potentially devastating and disabling trauma. Both during the years of turmoil and afterward, these practices of resilience have fostered the ongoing development of a communal faith narrative. That is, the Dinka have a particular way of understanding how God has worked through the Lost Boys to bring peace, stability, and hope to Southern Sudan. Their participation in God's redemptive work has left them with a deep sense of agency, purpose, and meaning. It is nothing short of a salvation narrative that provides the ultimate layer of resilience by pouring meaning into the life of suffering endured by the Lost Boys and other Dinka.

Through this story, I also wish to provide a model for how we, in our own congregations and communities, can offer practices of mutual care that may likewise sustain us through crisis and minimize the negative effects of traumatic experience.

To explore these practices further, I will also consider two broader issues. First, as anyone who has met the Lost Boys will already suspect, to understand the nature of any practice in the Dinka/Lost Boy community, one must examine how their Christian faith intersects with the deep traditions of that community. What we will find is that the structures that have framed Dinka spiritual healing for generations also frame their Christian faith. Second, to appreciate the resilience fostered by the Lost Boy community in the face of their traumatic experiences, we must critically examine the Western biomedical assumptions that currently dominate the global response to refugee trauma. While I do wish to explore how communal practices mitigate the effects of trauma, I do not want to do so from a purely individual and therapeutic perspective. Ultimately, the Lost Boys provide a fundamental model for the broader concept of creating a resilient community in the face of violence.

Pastoral Theology

I locate this inquiry within the Western discipline of pastoral theology and its practice of pastoral care. Christian pastoral theology largely, though not exclusively, tries to reconcile human experience, especially suffering, with the expectations of faith lived and revealed through the Christian tradition in light of the fragility and limitedness of the embodied human creature and the unyielding and unpredictable realities of the lived world toward an end of hope and meaning. Traditionally, pastoral theology has sought to explore human experience through the dual lenses of theology and psychology. The last two decades or so, however, have thankfully seen the emergence of culture as an essential third lens. Typically, any effort to provide appropriate pastoral care means untangling a complicated knot of psychological influences, residual emotions, underlying theologies, and cultural assumptions at work within individuals and their families and is a precarious task at best. It is even more complex when we examine the care and function of entire communities.

Traditional venues for the practice of pastoral theology include the local church in the care of a congregation, hospital chaplaincy, and pastoral counseling. Most recent paradigms expand the practice of pastoral theology and pastoral care to include both laypersons and the community at large as caregivers. Attention to the communal and contextual aspects of care, often referred to as the communal contextual paradigm based on John Patton's defining work in the late 1990s, helped shift the focus from individual to communal care.[1] The field continues to define the nuances of this paradigm, and I will push at the existing boundaries as well. For example, though the Lost Boys are devout in their faith and I wish to frame their practices as a model for the local church, they are not a traditional faith community as we have generally come to understand it. In fact, we may be tempted to consider them a secular group. By stepping into another culture to ask what we might learn from it, I join a select few other scholars who push the communal contextual paradigm into the global arena. Finally, though I will explore this issue less than others in the book, this research makes a case for moving American pastoral theology into unlikely places, such as war zones and refugee camps. We have something to offer these communities, just as they have much to offer us.

Indeed, pastoral theology provides a means of articulating and enhancing practices and challenges already faced by many faith-based nongovernmental organizations (NGOs) as they care for displaced persons and refugees around the world. Through such encounters, the people whom we seek to help also invite us to self-critique and growth. Even in our own cities, as we recognize the ever-increasing participa-

1. Patton, *Pastoral Care*, 6.

tion of immigrants and refugees, the discipline of pastoral theology has much to offer and to gain in the face of growing challenges.

A Word on Method

This research was obtained primarily through traditional, "feet-on-the-ground" ethnography. Borrowing from philosopher Gilbert Ryle, anthropologist Clifford Geertz defines *ethnography* simply as "thick description" but goes on to frame the doing of ethnography as "like trying to read . . . a manuscript—foreign, faded, full of ellipses, incoherencies, suspicious emendations, and tendentious commentaries, but written not in conventionalized graphs of sound but in transient examples of shaped behavior."[2] Since Geertz, numerous disciplines have adopted the term *thick description* to exposit identified behaviors within a given context and meaning.

This book is not only a thick description of who the Dinka are, but in many ways it is also an ethnography of suffering and resilience. By offering a thick description of the most important aspects of Dinka life that profoundly shape their identity, we can begin to understand how they interpret the losses resulting from war and displacement that create the most suffering. Though we often assume a shared knowledge across cultures of what constitutes a suffering event, in truth the depth of what causes pain and how one stays resilient in the face of it can only be understood in its cultural context.

I began working with Sudanese refugees in the spring of 2000 when I was in graduate school and serving in an extension ministry appointment with Catholic Charities Refugee Resettlement Program in Nashville, Tennessee. My primary task was to work as a liaison between refugees and local congregations who agreed to support them in the first months after arrival. In 2001, Catholic Charities, along with many other agencies around the country, began the process of resettling a group of refugees designated as unaccompanied minors (even though many were by then young adults) from Sudan called the Lost Boys. We had been warned by resettlement agencies, based on the circumstances of the boys' flight and displacement, that many were likely to suffer from posttraumatic stress disorder (PTSD). What became most noticeable, however, was not the level of dysfunction among the young

2. Geertz, *The Interpretation*, 10.

men but the high degree of resilience they displayed. True, they spoke of experiencing many effects associated with PTSD such as flashbacks and nightmares from the war, sleeplessness, and various somatic complaints. Yet, contrary to the debilitating effects one might expect from PTSD, it did not prevent them from very successfully acculturating to American life, obtaining employment, learning English, and going to high school (some even to college).[3] Research suggests that for many in this group, whatever effects of traumatic experience they suffered were mitigated by their connection to the community of other Lost Boys, the drive toward education instilled by their elders, and their faith in God.[4] I would add to this, more specifically, that participation in a communal faith narrative is a key resilience factor that brings meaning to otherwise devastating experiences.

These young refugees were the focus of my early research.[5] Many were connected through kinship to the Abang community, who make up the communal case study for this book. Very early in my work I realized that to better understand some of the traumatic circumstances they faced, to the degree that it is possible, it would be helpful to see the conditions in the refugee camp where they lived in limbo for so long during the war. Then, should a sustainable ceasefire emerge between the North and South, it would also be beneficial to venture inside Southern Sudan to see and experience the place they call home.

Indeed, in 2003, I traveled to Kakuma Refugee Camp in Kenya to meet family and clan members of the refugees I knew in Nashville and to observe firsthand the desperate conditions of life as a refugee. With a ceasefire finally holding in Southern Sudan, I received funding in 2008 from the Lilly Foundation and the MacMillan Center for International and Area Studies at Yale University to conduct research with refugees repatriated to Bor, in Southern Sudan. This book reflects information gleaned from interviews on this recent research trip, though the context

---

3. Goodman, "Coping," 1177–96; United States Department of Health, "Office of Refugee Resettlement Annual Report."

4. Goodman, "Coping," 1188–90; Luster et al., "The Lost Boys," 208; Schweitzer et al., "Coping," 285.

5. This research spans a period of eight years and includes my observations, information from scholarly and autobiographical texts, and material from group interviews with refugees in Bor, South Sudan.

is more broadly informed by my other experiences of learning among this population.

My greatest concern in the development of this research project with the Sudanese refugees has been their physical and emotional safety. In this regard, all interviews for this book adhered to the protocol approved by the Human Subjects Committee of the Institutional Review Board at Yale University. Consent was obtained and a translator was used to ensure that all participants understood the purpose and voluntary nature of the interviews, and that they could cease to participate at any time. No adverse effects of the interviews were reported to me. On the contrary, interviewees often exhorted me to "tell the world our story," indicating that the opportunity to tell their story may have even had some positive effect.[6]

Field research under harsh conditions, particularly in postconflict lands prone to ongoing violence, can present unique challenges to the traditional researcher-interviewee relationship. In many respects, including education, profession, income, nationality, and race, I held a position of privilege. This required that I consciously strive to be aware of its impact on my relationships and the interview process. I also recognized, however, that at certain times I was simultaneously dependent upon members of the local population, including those I interviewed, for, among other things, insider knowledge of which places were safe and which were not. This included knowledge of places susceptible to both armed intertribal violence and natural dangers. They, for example, guided me to outlying areas and had eyes to see snakes and other deadly creatures in the swampy brush that I did not. On more than one occasion, locals intervened to prevent injury to me.

My multiple professional roles, that is, as researcher, teacher, and clergy, presented further challenges. In a manner perhaps unique to pastoral theology, I was frequently asked to step into the role of clergy or pastor, sometimes without much preparation. For example, while interviewing two teachers in a remote village, I was told of the death the previous day of a three-year-old from typhoid. In the middle of the interview, I was asked to accompany the teachers to the girl's home and pray with the parents. In this culture, my job asking questions as a

6. Elizabeth Wood, professor of political science specializing in research in conflict zones, notes receiving a similar response from members of the community while gathering data in El Salvador during the war (Wood, "The Ethical Challenges," 378).

researcher did not preclude a pastoral visit to the small graveside and the home of these grieving parents. To refuse would have been a cultural and pastoral insult and quite unthinkable.

Lastly, I was on all fronts (emotionally, physically, theologically, and culturally) challenged by the field conditions, the social context, and the content of the interviews. The personal stories of the suffering that accompany two decades of war were difficult to hear. The poverty and everyday invitations to despair left me heavy of heart. The nearly 100-degree heat, constant negotiation of logistics, and my own sense of displacement were stressful and tiresome. I was constantly parsing my own personal response to their theology and the difficult cultural role of women while trying to remain respectful of the Dinka view of God and the world. Elizabeth Wood, writing about the ethics of research in conflict zones, notes, "Those carrying out extended field research in conflict zones are likely to experience additional and intense emotions in the course of their work, including fear, anger, outrage, grief, and pity, often through observing, suffering, or fearing the effects of violence."[7] The sum total of the experience left me drained. I tried to be aware of this and to use caution in interpreting my immediate reactions to people, encounters, and circumstances. These conditions plus the intercultural nature of the research cause me to continue to verify my impressions with contacts from the community when possible, to be cautious in my conclusions, and to lead with the question: how could I be wrong?

The Dinka and the Lost Boys

The Dinka tribe is one of the largest in Southern Sudan. Though I use the generic term *Dinka*, it should be noted that there are ten subdivisions of the tribe. Refugees in the United States, to accommodate those who are not privy to their intricate cultural specifics, generally condense their tribal affiliation to Dinka, though in their homeland further distinction is always necessary. In this book, I am speaking primarily of the Dinka Bor. Much of the research was conducted in the Abang community, which is a kinship group (clan) within the Dinka Bor, who mostly live within a self-defined geographical area in Bor and the outlying countryside. While in the countryside the Abang attend the village church, though when in the town of Bor they may visit different

7. Ibid., 384.

congregations. Nonetheless, they consider themselves to be one distinct community of faith.

The Lost Boys are young men mostly from the Dinka tribe who fled from their war-torn villages in 1989–1990.[8] These children, most between five and fifteen years old, fled across more than five hundred miles of desert unaccompanied by adults while facing constant threat of death from gunfire, wild animals, starvation, and disease. In 2000, the international community began to resettle these boys, now young men. Approximately 3,500 obtained permanent-resident status in the United States.

It is important to take a moment to comment on the term *Lost Boys*. This name was first given to these refugees by aid workers and the media when they were young boys fleeing the war in Sudan. Popular myth proposes that they were named so after the Lost Boys in the children's tale *Peter Pan* by James M. Barrie. I find the term problematic. On the one hand, it has been used rather effectively to garner funding and political support that ultimately facilitated the relocation of the young men to the United States and elsewhere. But the term also has a pejorative connotation that continues to paint (particularly to Westerners) an image of helpless orphaned boys, when in fact they are actually intelligent, resilient young men now building new lives. The refugees themselves are ambivalent about the term, recognizing that they have benefited from being called Lost Boys but knowing also that it does not define the essence of who they have become. Nonetheless, I use the term throughout this book primarily for the sake of consistency and because it is also a highly recognizable identifier for this refugee population.

West Is Best, Or Is It?

Most refugees embrace, at least to some degree, Western biomedical and psychodynamic intervention. Lost Boys, for example, readily accept its practices. Upon their arrival in the United States, they showed little fear or uncertainty when referred to a doctor or prescribed medication for a physical ailment. Likewise, there was also little resistance when medication was prescribed for those few who exhibited psychological

---

8. The Lost Boys I met through the resettlement process in Nashville come from many regions of southern Sudan, not only the Abang community.

symptoms that interfered with day-to-day functioning. In fact, they demanded such medical treatment for any and all maladies. Similarly, they readily acknowledged the term *trauma* and upon inquiry would tender a textbook definition (using Western vernacular) of PTSD's symptoms and causes. But how did this reliance develop when Western medicine was generally unavailable in the remote areas of Sudan from which the young men fled?

As mentioned, in 2003, I visited Kakuma Refugee Camp, located fifty kilometers south of the Sudanese border in Kenya, where the Lost Boys lived prior to resettlement in the United States. Of the 80,000 refugees living in this camp, the United Nations High Commissioner for Refugees (UNHCR) estimates that 75 percent have fled the conflict in Sudan. Another 25 percent come from surrounding countries. Aid agencies responsible for health and psychological services in the camp, though severely limited in resources, follow Western approaches to treatment of disease and mental illness. In spite of this dependence upon Western practices, there is a severe scarcity of professional physicians and even fewer trained psychologists or psychiatrists. In fact, during my visit, there was only one psychologist with a PhD, one master's-level psychologist, and one licensed psychiatrist (MD) to serve all 85,000 refugees. I make this observation not because I believe PhDs in psychology, psychiatrists, or medical doctors are the only qualified resources for healing. Rather, I state it as evidence that even though camp authorities espouse Western biomedical paradigms, they lack the resources necessary to render such models effective for such a large population. Most mental health services and some medical services in the camp are provided by laypersons. I will discuss the refugee camp environment more at a later point. Here I wish to focus on one observation. Though larger cities in Kenya and even Sudan offer some level of medical intervention, it seems likely that exposure to Western biomedical practices in the refugee camp supplies an explanation for the ready acceptance of Western medicine demonstrated by the refugees arriving in Nashville. Sadly, this acceptance of the biomedical culture has been accompanied by very little understanding of its limitations.

It is a great tragedy that though the Dinka have a long history of traditional healing methods, after exposure to Christian missionaries and ten years in Kakuma Refugee Camp, most now eschew traditional rituals in favor of Western medicine and models of psychodynamic therapy—even if they are unavailable. Traditional healing, generally speaking, is no longer considered to be effective except by those living in remote areas of Sudan. Nor is it considered appropriate for Christians to utilize such methods. Upon even the slightest investigation, the problem becomes obvious: while their richest resource (namely, the refugees and their traditions) remains all too plentiful, Western medicine is in dangerously short supply.

This is precisely why understanding how the Lost Boys practice such powerful care with one another is invaluable. In spite of minimal medical or psychological intervention, they have, I suggest, largely managed to mitigate what Western psychological models of care would call symptoms of PTSD. They have done this by modeling their community practices on those learned through generations of spiritual healing traditions and their own faith.

Turning the Tables: What Do the Lost Boys Have to Teach Us?

Ten years ago, the connection between trauma, the practices of the Lost Boys, and the behavior of our own communities might have been more difficult to see. But Columbine, 9/11, Virginia Tech, Katrina, and the Iraq War have brought the reality of trauma to our own backyard in such a way that we can more easily see a glimpse of our circumstances reflected in those of the Lost Boys.

Appreciating their concept of community, however, is a bit more complicated. Americans have an ambiguous notion of community. On the one hand, most Americans make strong claims about deep connections to family, community, and nation. Yet a high sense of individualism and a capitalist economy virtually ensure the strongly competitive nature of American culture. Indeed, Americans are often characterized as living in competition with our neighbors. The phrase "keeping up with the Joneses" is a common expression that indicates the overwhelming need to have at least as much as our neighbor has. In his book *Falling Behind: How Rising Inequality Harms the Middle Class*, Robert Franks proposes that the superconsumer environment in the United States is, not surprisingly, negatively affecting social norms.[9] He points to the avoidance of *relative deprivation* as the core source of behavior

9. Franks, *Falling Behind*.

that compels most of us not only to desire what our neighbors have but to live at a level beyond while lording it over them in the process.

The Lost Boys teach us that behavior such as this is not just an economic issue but an ethical one. Cultural and religious tradition teaches the Lost Boys that the only acceptable social norm is, indeed, that one should have as much as his or her neighbor but only as much. In fact, the ethical demand among these Sudanese is that each person should *help* the Joneses keep up with them! This is fundamental to their concepts of safety and justice. To live beyond the means of one's neighbor—to watch them do without—is morally reprehensible. Imagine the value of this social mandate in times of crisis such as war, famine, or displacement when external resources are overwhelmed or nonexistent. This code that honors one's neighbor forms the moral foundation of care and obligation that sustains and strengthens the Lost Boy community.

It is only fair to point out that in spite of the evidence to the contrary, this concept of community care is not foreign to Americans, particularly among those who participate in a faith community. Nor should I leave you with the impression that the Lost Boys (or the greater Sudanese community) negotiate living up to this vision of community in anything other than sometimes-messy, imperfect, and utterly human ways. I do suggest that whereas North Americans tend to separate the secular and religious, the Lost Boys do not separate the community of faith from the everyday, face-to-face community. Ultimately, this is how the Lost Boys have created a healing community—one from which we, no matter how different the culture, can learn

Overview

Chapter 1 will elaborate the communal contextual and intercultural paradigms in pastoral theology and discuss the ways in which they are challenged and enhanced by the model of community demonstrated by the Lost Boys. I will also explore the particular ways that pastoral theology is especially adept at providing a means to understanding how to hold both the wounds of traumatic experience and resilience from traumatic experience in appropriate tension with culture and faith. I will explore the interdisciplinary history of resilience theory, including more recent uses of it in disaster recovery. This will open a conversation that addresses how the concept of resilience can serve the discipline of pastoral theol-

ogy and pastoral care as well as the distinctive contribution religious faith
might make to actual resilience within a traumatized community.

Chapter 2 examines the political and social context for the lives
of the Lost Boys. It gives a very brief review of the turbulent history of
Sudan, especially from 1960 to the present, and considers the conflict
between the North and South in terms of religious, political, and ethnic
differences. This chapter also highlights the impact of slavery and famine, especially when used as tools of war, on the South. It will explore
traditions of the Dinka tribe to which the Lost Boys belong in terms of
familial relationships, including kinship, food rituals, their relationship
to cattle, and rites of passage—noting where appropriate how tactics of
war have negatively affected these traditions.

The term *Lost Boy* is itself a reflection of the traumatic experiences
a large group of Dinka children faced during the civil war in Sudan. In
chapter 3, using the personal narratives of Lost Boy refugees, I will describe the traumatic events they endured in a one-thousand-kilometer
journey from their home villages in Southern Sudan to Ethiopia, then
again across Sudan to a decade of living in a refugee camp. How they
understand the role of faith in their survival will begin to become apparent. Here I will also introduce how what we would call traumatic
symptoms present themselves in the lives of these refugees.

Chapter 4 briefly examines the formal *Diagnostic and Statistic
Manual of Mental Disorders* (4th ed.) diagnosis of posttraumatic stress
disorder and critiques its use as a diagnostic tool in refugee populations. I will address how some traditional interpretations of trauma and
resources for healing (including religious faith) among refugee populations are discouraged or dismissed in favor of Western diagnoses and
therapeutic treatments. The ramification of such a bias will become
clear. This will prepare readers for a subsequent discussion about the
evidence of the resilient nature of the Lost Boys.

One of the most remarkable aspects of the Lost Boy population
is their resourcefulness in the face of what could be considered overwhelming trauma. Chapter 5 will explore how Dinka traditions have
informed and been transformed by their Christian faith to provide a
communal model of healing for the Lost Boys. Here we discover what
has helped them create a community framed by care and obligation that
consequently provides a relatively safe holding place, articulates justice,
and creates a collective trauma narrative. Ultimately, it is these practices

of care exhibited by the Lost Boys that created an environment able to mitigate some of the most debilitating of traumatic symptoms.

Chapter 6 introduces the communal faith narrative, the horizon toward which all other obligations of care move and in which they find their ultimate fulfillment. It is their deepest source of resilience and the theological frame through which the Dinka understand God at work to bring peace, healing, and progress to Southern Sudan. As people who live in the shade of Christ's redemptive promise, the Dinka find a sense of purpose, meaning, and even agency through this faith narrative.

Learning from a resilience model highlights strengths as resources that may otherwise be overlooked. It is my hope that this unique opportunity to learn from a remarkable group of refugees, the Lost Boys, will offer a new perspective on how to create a resilient community teeming with hidden resources.

1

Shifting Perspectives in Pastoral Theology

When one has nothing in this desolate place the choice is simple: believe in a God who will provide or give oneself over to despair. The Dinka I have met in Southern Sudan have decided to believe in a God who, against all odds, will provide. Already in this small outpost town, there are more than twenty-five churches. Not one has anything but a bare earthen floor or walls made of anything but mud. Some have shiny corrugated aluminum roofs strong enough to withstand the long rainy season; others make do with patchwork plastic or a roof woven together like a bird's nest that must be replaced every dry season. There are no brass crosses to sit atop shiny altars but only a drum and offering basket to take center stage. Have no doubt, though, these are proud houses of worship for hundreds if not thousands on Sunday morning. We make our way to the church by following a sea of colored plastic chairs bobbing atop the heads of tall dark-skinned Dinka. We forgot to bring our chairs. No matter, we are embarrassingly ushered forward to visitors' seats in the front. So much for the anonymity of the back pew! I feel shabby in my dusty boots and field clothes compared to the clean pressed shirts and brightly colored African dresses with head-scarves. The overflow listens from outside the church and only nursing mothers move inside when the rains begin. They have come to hear the Word and hear it they will. Only in Word and prayer do they find hope for another day.

—Field notes from Bor, Sudan

FROM THE EARLIEST DAYS OF MY CAREER AS AN ACADEMIC, I have been pursuing the question of trauma and resilience in communities afflicted with violence and disaster. How, I ask, can people in utterly devastating circumstances manage not only to persevere but even to thrive? I recall the woman in August of 1996 standing in front of a block of buildings decimated by the shelling in Sarajevo—only a façade stood to reveal what used to be a row of shops and apartments. Steadily, she swept the dust from a large square portion of the sidewalk in front of the mine-filled rubble. Why? Was this madness at work or some small effort to bring order to the chaos of war's aftermath? Elsewhere, in the Palestinian village of Samu in late 1996, how did the children make sense of the armed soldiers patrolling the streets under full "lockdown"—shut off from the world and all deliveries of food and water? On yet another continent, how did the father in Estelí, Nicaragua, who watched his son die after being buried nearly to the neck in a mudslide after Hurricane Mitch in 1998, rally to provide for and comfort the living children still by his side? And then there are the children of Sudan, whom we will meet shortly. There is no shortage of tragedy from war and natural disaster around the globe. Though the above are only brief anecdotal glimpses of the resilience I have encountered, they speak to what compels me toward the research I do.

In each of these cases, I witnessed a powerful ability of people to overcome circumstances that could have just as easily rendered them immobilized and helpless. They focused, instead, on feeding their families, rebuilding their homes, finding work, getting married, and having children. In some cases, the violence continued in one form or another. But they pressed on. It was as if no one told them they were supposed to be undone by the terrible things they had experienced. The resilience I witnessed, interestingly enough, did not preclude many from also experiencing what we would call traumatic symptoms, some of which may have caused periods of distress. Unfortunately, it was these symptoms only upon which psychosocial service agencies and other medical personnel focused.

When focusing on the pathology of trauma, Western care professionals pay little heed to the resources for resilience. A recent conversation with a medical colleague concerning informed consent among refugees from war provides a glimpse into the thinking behind psychological care in communities of other (non-Western) cultures. She stated that the Dinka, for example, are not informed enough (implying lack of Western medical knowledge) to give consent; after all, they don't know about posttraumatic stress disorder (PTSD) and don't realize what may happen if they start talking about past events. The assumption here, of course, is that individuals who have lived under conditions of war for two decades don't understand what might happen if they talk about what they have experienced, or, more important, that they lack the ability to make a judgment about whether it would cause them harm to do so. It never occurred to her that people living at war for twenty years may actually know *more* than she about what happens when one talks about these difficult things. In my experience, this attitude is pervasive and trickles down through aid programs so that the refugee experience is dismissed in favor of Western biomedical paradigms.

In remote communities and refugee camps, a common strategy of care in response to trauma has been to train laypersons to practice basic counseling skills. These skills are specifically oriented toward the symptoms of Western definitions of posttraumatic stress disorder. Little or no attention is given to aspects of community or faith, both of which are essential resources in many cultural contexts. Though training booklets given out during my visit to Nicaragua, for example, had been translated into Spanish, the curriculum gave scant attention to any other aspect of the context in which it was applied. In Kakuma refugee camp (Kenya), training for this method of individually focused talk "therapy" also overlooked significant aspects of community, faith, and tradition unique to Sudan and the Dinka.

Indeed, community and faith are two significant sources of resilience that become quick casualties of Western approaches to healing. In Central American and African contexts especially, the effects of violent conflict or disaster are felt most deeply within the communal structure. Members of the community often express loss in terms of how it relates to family, clan, and neighbor; the individual stands primarily as an extension of these. In this context, highly individualistic therapeutic strategies make little sense; nonetheless, aid organizations continue to import them. Psychosocial professionals, in general, give little regard to religious faith as part of the treatment strategy for trauma among refugees, yet it is one of the most consistent resources for nearly all of the individuals and communities I visited. So, how can pastoral theology help address this lack of attention to cultural context in the treatment of trauma?

I have approached this study of the Lost Boys through a culturally-critical pastoral theological method in an effort to broker a better understanding of how this community has acted to mitigate the sometimes debilitating psychological symptoms associated with what is often diagnosed as PTSD. Here I will bring together three lenses (the cultural critique of anthropology, theology, and psychology) through which to sharpen a pastoral theological focus on the Lost Boy community and traumatic experience.

Arthur Kleinman, anthropologist and psychiatrist, provides an interesting glimpse into how Western biomedical practices separate personal narrative from an illness event, thus taking it out of the context of individual lives. He has written extensively in the area of medical anthropology and has added significantly to our understanding of how what we call depression manifests itself in other cultures. Kleinman challenges the biomedical community to understand illness and healing within the context of a patient's own cultural perspective. This emphasis on cultural narrative is of immense value in interpreting and treating refugees, who often face a multitude of physical and psychological challenges.

Kleinman contributes three important thoughts in this regard. First, in *The Illness Narratives*, he proposes a tripartite understanding of what is commonly known as an illness episode. Kleinman defines *illness* as the experience of the symptoms that include not only the physical aspects of disease but also the emotional, interpersonal, and economic consequences as well; *disease* denotes the biomedical interpretation of illness symptoms; and *sickness* is the cultural interpretation of the disease.[1] The way a family member will describe the impact of a particular illness is not necessarily the same as how a physician will describe its impact as a disease.

Kleinman goes on to propose four levels of meaning behind every illness event. These include the *first level*, how the individual understands the symptoms of a disease in relation to his or her body, self, and society. *Second* is the cultural level that gives particular meaning to certain diseases and symptoms (cancer, AIDS, even PTSD). How symptoms relate to the web of relationships that make up an individual's

---

1. Kleinman, *The Illness Narratives*, 32–53.

personal world is the *third* level of meaning. Finally, the *fourth* level is the clinical meaning of the disease—what Kleinman calls the "clinical reality."[2] These layers of meaning, as understood from the perspective of the patient, come to constitute an explanatory model of illness that is often presented, he claims, in the form of personal, or I would add communal, narrative.[3] As we will see, narratives, especially faith narratives, have, indeed, become an essential source of resilience for the Dinka.

Pushing at the Boundaries

In some ways, this ethnographic study of how a group of war-ravaged Sudanese refugees find resilience through communal obligation and a shared faith narrative feels like a bit of an anomaly for the discipline of pastoral theology. And yet the two reigning paradigms in pastoral theology, the communal contextual and the intercultural, invite just such an inquiry.

In the early 1990s, John Patton proposed that pastoral care was a task for the community of faith (i.e., not reserved for ordained clergy). He compared pastoral caregivers to "mini-ethnographers" who must explore the particularities of context in every care encounter.[4] Within the next decade, the intercultural paradigm also emerged and challenged pastoral theology to do the difficult work of considering the alternate worldviews and systems of influence rising from different cultures.

These conflicted feelings, that this research is both an anomaly and quite at home in pastoral theology, indicate the sense of both belonging and alienation that often occurs when one pushes against familiar boundaries in order to embrace a new perspective.

In 2006, the Society for Pastoral Theology met in Denver, Colorado, for its annual meeting. That year the theme of the study conference was violence. We visited the nearby area of Columbine—site of the horrific school shooting in 1999 that resulted in the murder of thirteen students and faculty, the suicide of the two perpetrators, and the wounding of dozens. Several survivors and family members graciously spoke with us. The pain and feelings of loss were quite palpable even seven years after the event. Though individual stories framed our time together,

2. Ibid., 49, 121.
3. Ibid., 125.
4. Patton, *Pastoral Care*, 43.

the narratives made it clear that the shooting was a communal trauma. We were, of course, particularly interested to learn about how the community of faith (broadly speaking) and local church congregations responded. These, it turned out, were deeply interwoven with the needs and responses of the larger Columbine and Littleton communities. Hearing their stories, I began to consider how traumatic crisis causes the boundaries, as we define them, between a community of faith and the many other levels of community to shift and blur. I experienced a similar blurring of communal boundaries while visiting the town of Bor in Sudan. The crisis of war caused the defining edges of kinship, community of faith, and neighbor to blend and move with the vulnerabilities from the ongoing conflict and the deep sense of suffering.

John Patton describes a paradigm shift in pastoral care from the clinical to the communal contextual paradigm when he speaks of "[broadening] the focus of pastoral care beyond the individual pastor to the larger group of carers within the Christian community."[5] He uses the metaphor of remembering in two ways, that of God's remembering, which brings us together in human relationship, and re-membering, or the re-visioning of community when considered in a particular context.[6] I would like to suggest a third aspect of re-membering especially appropriate to the context of trauma, that is, the task of bringing together again the community after it has been broken and scattered by violence and loss. This remembering and re-membering is the heart of the caring ecclesial community but extends beyond to the greater community. It is the root of a moral obligation to care, and something the Dinka of Sudan understand well. As we will see, the story of the Dinka is one about how a community of faith (albeit one defined a bit differently from that of our local congregation) creates an ethos of care in times of great spiritual and psychological crisis. To do this, they call on a moral obligation of care passed down through generations of familial tradition as well as a similar moral obligation rooted in the Christian imperative to love and care for one another.

While the communal, contextual paradigm has largely been used to explore the ways laity participate in pastoral care within the local church community, I wish to push this definition toward a more

5. Ibid., 6, 15.

6. Ibid., 7.

interconnected vision of care. Building on her idea of the "living human web" as the subject matter of pastoral theology,[7] Bonnie Miller-McLemore has described care in this way: "Genuine care now requires understanding the human document as necessarily embedded within an interlocking public web of constructed meaning."[8] How, for example, might the community of faith participate in building a collective spiritual resilience within the congregation? Further, large-scale violence and disaster such as school shootings and terrorist attacks have made us ask, how do we care for the larger community in light of such trauma and suffering? Not long after the attacks on September 11, Howard Clinebell posted the following comments:

> 9/11, the 'day that changed the world,' pushed me harder than ever before to ask myself yet again: What is the missing piece in facilitating holistic healing of collective trauma and systemic grief? . . . [T]he challenge of 9/11 for pastoral caregivers is immense and many faceted. Let's hope that we who are trained to think in disciplined ways about cultivating spiritually-centered, holistic healing will use this window of opportunity to make innovative discoveries of healing modalities for countless wounded persons and families but also for our deeply and collectively wounded nation and global community.[9]

Larry Kent Graham, addressing the same meeting of the Society for Pastoral Theology in Colorado, likewise observes,

> The ongoing threat and reality of terrorism, genocide, and other forms of Democide, expose us to the increasing possibility of public tragedy and corporate grief . . . These events call for deeper analysis as well as generative networks of prevention, when possible, and response. They also reveal deep fissures and seemingly irrevocable differences in the human family. In the face of these and other catastrophes and the rising threat of new disasters, pastoral caregivers and their teachers and supervisors are called upon for guidance, interpretation, wisdom, and compassion."[10]

7. Miller-McLemore, "The Living Human Web," 16.

8. Ibid., 51.

9. Clinebell, "Pastoral Caregivers."

10. Graham, "Pastoral Theology and Catastrophic Disaster," 1–2.

Can the communal contextual paradigm help us push the boundaries to move between the community of faith into the general community, moving beyond individual stories of trauma (sustained through abuse, sexual violence, and combat, for example) to examine how the community collectively experiences and recovers from traumatic events?

Global Dimensions of Pastoral Theology, Care, and Counseling

The time I spend in cultures other than my own (the culture of the United States)—especially my research time in Sudan—presses me to explore how pastoral theology continues to redefine itself within the intercultural paradigm. Several questions rise to the surface that help me explore what I will call the global dimensions of the intercultural paradigm. They include: 1. What do we mean by intercultural care? 2. How do we relate our own issues of suffering to those of the global community (including the developing world)? 3. How does Western pastoral care relate to pastoral care across our borders? What notions of entitlement do we carry with us as we relate to other cultures? 4. How can we learn from care practices from other cultures?

What *do* we mean by *intercultural*? How we use the term *intercultural* in pastoral theology, care, and counseling is rather complex. While the paradigm itself covers a broad scope, the term *intercultural* is often used to examine care for individuals whose culture of location is the United States, but who claim a different culture of origin or ancestry. In other words, it addresses the intercultural within the boundaries of the United States. To be sure, this is of monumental importance; it raises the question of difference and has made room for brilliant work in Womanist and African American pastoral theology as well as work among Korean, Latino/a, and other communities.

It is less often used to describe a cross-cultural exchange of care that moves across national or geographic borders, or to explore ways we can learn from caring communities in other cultures around the world. In the end, this notion of learning about care from another culture in another part of the world—especially from among those considered to be the least educated and most marginalized—is the point where this research pushes against the edges of what we know as the intercultural paradigm. When we cross borders and plant our feet in other lands not to impose our practices but to *learn* about pastoral care, we engage in not only intercultural but also global dimension of pastoral care. This is the aspect of the intercultural paradigm upon which I will focus my attention.

Bringing attention back to the questions at hand, one can see an emerging engagement with global concerns in pastoral theology over the last two decades. Let me say from the start that this brief glimpse of how scholars in the field of pastoral theology, care, and counseling have engaged global concerns in the recent past presents a very limited view. It is far from exhaustive, and many fine scholars, articles, and books are left unmentioned. Nonetheless, even this brief sketch will help identify the places where my research engages both new questions and those already being asked about the global dimensions of pastoral theology, care, and counseling.

I have chosen the term *global dimension* of pastoral theology over *internationalization*, which has been used by some in our field.[11] This is a personal preference due largely to the particular population with whom I work: refugees. Intended or not, *international* less effectively represents the voiceless poor and marginalized than does the term *global*. Think of what we imagine when we hear about international relations, international negotiations, international business, international students, or even international pastoral care. In its common use *international* denotes those who, in the context of their meeting, stand on relatively equal ground (as professionals, students, etc.) while reaching across borders for a common purpose. I choose *global*, in spite of any unfortunate connotations it may carry, because of its relation to globalization, because it is generally more inclusive of the poor and marginalized, and, in my opinion, implies a more comprehensive worldwide vision.

David Augsberger in his book *Pastoral Counseling across Cultures* made a significant early contribution toward challenging pastoral theology and care in diverse cultural contexts. Other work, including the 1992 monograph *Therapeutic Practice in a Cross-Cultural World* out of the Danielsen Institute at Boston University, and published papers from the International Pastoral Care Network for Social Responsibility

11. See, for example, Nancy Ramsay, Pam Couture, and Emmanuel Lartey: Ramsay, "A Time of Ferment," 23; Couture and Lartey, "Pastoral Theology in International Perspective," v–vii; Lartey, "Globalization," 87–108.

conference in 1996, indicate the emerging questions concerning care in multiple ethnic contexts.

This question concerning the global dimension of pastoral theology, care, and counseling is not a new one. Emmanuel Lartey has long been at the forefront of this discussion. In his book *In Living Color* he provides us with a wonderful glimpse of pastoral care on the global stage when, adding to the classical history of the field, he includes contributions from theologians in two African nations, from Great Britain, and from the Islamic faith. He reminds us of the ongoing conversation among multiple cultures represented in the meeting of the International Congress (now Council) of Pastoral Care and Counseling.[12] Not only does he help us understand the different ways that pastoral theology is practiced in other cultures around the world, but he provides a glimpse of the ways these practices challenge American paradigms of pastoral theology, care, and counseling, which, like Western medical paradigms, have been exported as the standard practice. Perhaps most important, by framing care in terms of how people are like some others, all others, and no other, Lartey provides a methodology that helps us parse difference and sameness in intercultural care.[13]

Elsewhere, Lartey further offers a frame for understanding the relationship between Western pastoral-care theories and those from other cultures. He divides this frame into three levels: globalization (the practice of exporting Western paradigms such as stated above); internationalization (which recognizes culturally contextual differences and eschews claims of universal practices), and Indigenization (which makes a claim for the emergence of truly contextually driven theories and practices).[14] These categories are very helpful and make much room for discussion of how Western models in a Western context might be informed by practices of care from other cultures.

How we in the United States perceive the practices of non-Western cultures can be deeply influenced by underlying feelings of entitlement and superiority. Ryan LaMothe has taken on the important task of addressing the nature of the Christian church in relation to the deeply rooted, long-lived vision of "American Empire," that is, entitlement to

12. For more information on the International Council of Pastoral Care and Counseling (ICPCC), please consult their webpage: http://www.icpcc.net.

13. Lartey, *In Living Color*, 171.

14. Lartey, "Globalization," 88–91

economic, military, and political domination across the world.[15] He articulates the ways that Christian communities in the United States have colluded, on a highly internalized level, with the goals of American expansionism. This work brings pastoral theology into conversation with global concerns with respect to the question of what motivates American action in the world and how American Christian communities are complicit in the suffering such action inflicts. The underlying sense of entitlement LaMothe describes detrimentally impacts the willingness of communities of faith to learn from the rich resources of knowledge that other cultures offer. Ironically, understanding the effects of American Empire and pulling loose from the bonds of entitlement that snare us are challenges often accomplished most effectively when we experience worlds beyond our own.

And what do our worlds have in common? Though the particularities of suffering are specific to each context, suffering is a reality of the global community. I am suggesting that some aspects of violence, trauma, and, most important, resilience, are a shared global concern. A special issue of the *Journal of Pastoral Theology* titled *Pastoral Theology in International Perspective* was published in 2007, presenting papers from the same conference that included discussion on the Columbine shooting, and highlighted issues of violence affecting the global community. The issue is dedicated by its editors to the promotion of "global awareness and international pastoral responses."[16] Articles in this issue address topics essential to taking pastoral theology into the global arena, including a theological response to the conflict in the Democratic Republic of Congo, the global AIDS crisis, and the power of learning about ourselves when we immerse ourselves in another culture.

Others in pastoral theology have, likewise, begun to bring into focus concerns we share as a global community. In 2002, Sharon Thornton's *Broken yet Beloved: A Pastoral Theology of the Cross* highlighted the need for closer attention to the social context of suffering, and challenged cultural notions such as individualization and self-realization that often impede our understanding of cultures where the community is central to growth and flourishing. In 2007, Pamela Couture highlighted the interconnectedness of the global community in relation to the lives of children in her book *Child Poverty: Love, Justice, and*

15. LaMothe, *Empire Matters*, 61.

16. Couture and Lartey, "Pastoral Theology in International Perspective," v.

Social Responsibility. Here, she interweaves the complex issues affecting children across the nations, including war, human trafficking, and general economic instability. Couture has also written more specifically on war in the Democratic Republic of Congo and the resilience of a local church community in Kamina.[17] In her hearing of the story and providing the thick description necessary to understand the deep sources of suffering, Couture not only undertakes a pastoral-theological task, as she suggests, but also breaks open the global boundaries of care that have long prevented us from venturing across our borders.[18]

Resilience

As the title implies, resilience is of fundamental importance in this book. My surprise at the emotional and spiritual resourcefulness of refugees even in the earliest years of my work compelled a shift in perspective in the way I study trauma. Resilience is a good thing. Few would dispute this, I think. Often it is an end whose good is obvious enough that it is not necessary to articulate a specific definition. It is actually quite difficult to pull together words enough to cover the vastness of the impact resilience has on a life of suffering and despair. Just when I think I have defined my understanding of resilience in the context of the Dinka, I discover that my definition is lacking in some way or overly rigid so as to discount small but nonetheless essential efforts. So, I am left offering a working definition of resilience followed by a rationale for the importance of understanding resilience in this work and in pastoral theology, care, and counseling in general.

I use the term *resilience* to mean the ability not only to survive overwhelming threat or injury but also to engage strategies of coping that move one toward growth and flourishing. These strategies include behaviors, beliefs, and even physical attributes adopted or adapted by persons and communities under conditions of duress that serve to mitigate the negative experiences of suffering. These strategies are resilient only so long as they provide this mitigating effect while not also creating subsequent aspects of suffering for self or others. In other words, even resilient behaviors can become maladaptive when they no longer serve a positive function or take a turn toward creating additional suffering.

17. Couture, "Demystifying the War," 15–26.
18. Ibid., 16–17.

I wish to argue that if we look at the community of Lost Boys from a strength perspective, that is, from the perspective of resilience, then we are able to see a more complex system of responses to pervasive trauma. Not only does this liberate the Lost Boys from a simplistic victim role, but it opens the possibility that we might learn something about the resilient community that would prove helpful in our own culture.

I make the claim in this book that resilience has taken hold among the Dinka people largely because they have found a way to make meaning out of their own suffering. They do this through believing that God is working through them toward a purpose of goodness and healing. Perhaps, as James Poling suggests, their resilience reflects God's resilience, that is, "when God's power and goodness are compromised by evil, God does not give up. God continues to empower the world and continues to offer life and beauty when everything seems lost."[19] As the Dinka live into the space between their resilience and God's, the reality of suffering does not change; but its impact on individual and community does.

Perspective: Strength versus Deficit

Nearly twenty years, ago I quit smoking. In the effort to stave off the immediate craving for a cigarette triggered by sitting in my favorite chair, I rearranged the furniture. I was shocked by how a simple shift in perspective allowed me to see a very familiar space in a profoundly different way. Similarly, I have "rearranged the furniture" a bit in my approach to examining traumatic experience, particularly in the lives of refugees. Instead of focusing primarily on the pathology associated with PTSD and its clinical diagnosis that results from years of living under threat of violence and the ensuing loss of life, land, and sustenance, I wish to engage in the study of the prevailing characteristics of resilience. I do this for at least two reasons.

First, as suggested above, assumptions of universal pathology in an intercultural context such as Southern Sudan often lead to a distorted interpretation of what may be considered unhealthy behavior. This in turn undervalues effective resources of coping that lead to resilience. But the importance extends beyond this even to those in Western culture. Modern mental health paradigms are built on deficit models.

19. Poling, "Creativity," 101.

Simply put, when we are looking for pathology, we more often recognize failure than strength. In his study on stress, psychologist Stevan Hobfoll notes, "By focusing on illness, we accept dysfunction as the end point . . . by focusing on pathological outcomes, we end up with a 'crippled psychology.'"[20]

To complicate the matter, in the case of refugees and other marginalized populations dealing with trauma, effective treatment of pathology is traditionally framed in terms of pharmacological and other professional intervention (talk therapy), which is of limited availability and, if available, seldom affordable. Strength-based research, on the other hand, can highlight the effective use of available resources, internal and otherwise, that though often dismissed, can lead to resilience in the face of traumatic events. Subsequent large-scale support of these strength-enhancing resources in the community is one strategy toward building resilience.

I do not wish, through this book, to discount Western diagnostic methods and treatments for PTSD, or to make claims that they are ineffective or unnecessary, especially in Western culture. I do suggest, however, that the universal application of PTSD diagnosis and treatment methods in other cultures often undervalues and distorts practices and behaviors that may, in fact, serve to strengthen individuals in the face of ongoing violence. Even in our own culture, medical paradigms for understanding and treating PTSD have often negated the value of coping measures rooted in community, especially in the religious community. Furthermore, many people lack sufficient health insurance to seek mental health assistance, and even those with coverage may find mental health benefits limited. Public health clinics are notable for long waits that make follow-up care inconsistent and difficult. Whether or not one has private or public mental health assistance available to them, we must also deal with the stigma associated with seeking help for mental health issues.

In a time when violence seems to permeate our communities, it is becoming all the more essential that pastoral caregivers seek to understand ways that we can help communities healthfully create possibilities for resilience. In the context of the United States, this has become increasingly important since the events of September 11. Though there

---

20. Hobfoll, *Stress*, 167.

have certainly been significantly traumatic events before and since, 9/11 remains a pivotal moment in time for citizens in the United States. Since that day, fear of terrorism has become a shadow that hovers close, and trauma a part of the vernacular. In 2003, in response to September 11, Senator Patrick Kennedy introduced the National Resilience Development Act, which states one of its primary goals to be: "To coordinate the efforts of different government agencies in researching, developing, and implementing programs and protocols designed to increase the psychological resilience and mitigate distress reactions and maladaptive behaviors of the American public as they relate to terrorism."[21] Though this bill seems to have become lost in government bureaucracy, the sentiment is telling. Indeed, research in the last decade has begun to ask the question, what makes a community resilient?

Incorporating Suffering

The first issue I raised is one of perspective—strength versus deficit (pathology). The second involves the misconception that resilience means returning to a state of equilibrium unaffected by the suffering encountered along the way. Resilience from a pastoral-theological perspective makes no claim that one can ever return to a previous state of being but rather seeks to incorporate one's experiences, even experiences of suffering, into a positive process of meaning making. For our purposes in this book, resilience will be especially significant not as an ability to recover a previous state of equilibrium but as a capacity to proactively mitigate the effects of trauma to make them tolerable and engage in a process of meaning making that moves toward a hope-filled future.

A simple turn at the nearest dictionary offers an entirely insufficient definition of *resilience* for our purposes. It reads: "the capability of a strained body to recover its size and shape after deformation caused esp. by compressive stress," and "the ability to recover from or adjust easily to misfortune and change."[22] In a somewhat similar vein, ecological resilience is defined as the ability of an ecological system to withstand change, implying at least some retention of original form in

---

21. The last action on this bill occurred on June 25, 2003, when it was referred to the Subcommittee on Crime, Terrorism, and Homeland Security. Online: http://www .govtrack.us/congress/billtext.xpd?bill=h108-2370.

22. Woolf, *Webster's*, 977.

the face of either necessary or catastrophic change or interruption.[23] It is notable that these understandings of resilience seem to suggest that the ability to rebound may be a self-contained effort, *and* that the organism undergoes no permanent change.

Disciplines in the social sciences make use of *resilience* in slightly different ways, but all draw focus to the ways human beings cope with adverse conditions. One of the earlier studies on resilience in the field of mental health was conducted by Emmy Werner and Ruth Smith. This longitudinal study of children on the island of Kauai, Hawaii, covered nearly two decades and examined the children's abilities to cope with "perinatal stress, poverty, and parental psychopathology."[24] Though they were looking for pathology in the lives of children living under high-risk conditions, what they discovered was that some had a propensity for resilience and were better able to cope than others. Werner and Smith define *resilience* as "[the] capacity to cope effectively with the internal stresses of their vulnerabilities."[25]

The authors offer a glimpse into an unfortunate subtext to this definition in the title of their book, *Vulnerable but Invincible.* The implication seems to be that these children who persevered under extreme conditions were in some sense "invincible," as if they could deflect or remain uninfluenced by the chronic poverty and mental illness in their families. Yet every interaction with one's environment and other human beings creates a potential for change within us. Our perception of the world and our place in it is constantly being challenged and altered by human experience, especially traumatic experience.

I also want to consider here the connection between resistance and resilience. Resistance, pushing back against forces that oppress or wound, is a very important aspect of resilience that has been highlighted especially by feminist and womanist scholars. As I have worked on this book, kind colleagues have sent me articles, notes, and books about resilience. In the course of this generosity I have also received many notes about resistance—as if some had mistaken the topic of my work. This occurred frequently enough, though, that I came to recognize the act of substituting resistance for resilience as an indication of the deep connection many make between the two.

23. Folke et al., "Synthesis," 354.

24. Werner and Smith, *Vulnerable*, 6.

25 Ibid., 4.

Bonnie Miller-McLemore adds resistance, along with empowering, nurturing, and liberating—all of which are especially essential to the global dimension of pastoral theology and care—to the long-held classic pastoral-care functions of healing, sustaining, guiding, and reconciliation.[26] In the life of the Dinka and other refugees I have seen how communal acts of resistance literally help sustain life. For example, I visited Kakuma refugee camp (home to eighty thousand refugees) only one month before a census was due to be taken. It is necessary to count the actual persons in the camp in order to verify the number of food-ration cards used. This seems logical enough. However, as we will see shortly, the food rations in the camp were inadequate to meet basic needs. Refugees who left the camp for visits to other cities, or those resettled elsewhere, would therefore give their ration cards to a family member or friend before departure. A census would invalidate those extra cards. The previous attempt at a census resulted in riots by the refugees. In this case, violence was the only resource of resistance available to the refugees to prevent the governing system from reducing their only source of sustenance. Though we in pastoral theology often speak of the power of nonviolent resistance as it confronts violence, in the upside-down world of the refugee there are times when the choice is violence or starvation. In these times, violence can be an act of resistance and resilience.

Froma Walsh, a clinical psychologist who specializes in family resilience, notes that this idea of being invincible or rebounding gives a false impression that resilience means not being affected by suffering. This, she says, leads to the idea that resilience is a matter of innate strength versus weakness, in which one should be tough enough that suffering and hardship roll off our backs and leave us unfazed by the experience. Walsh goes so far as to suggest that this dichotomy of strong versus weak leads to a "culture that breeds intolerance for personal suffering,"[27] and urges us to "simply put national crises and past atrocities behind us . . . without looking back to draw meaning from them, come to terms with them, and heal as a society."[28] A more helpful understanding of resilience is one in which an individual (or, I would

26. Miller-McLemore, "Feminist Theory," 80.

27. Walsh, *Strengthening Family Resilience*, 7.

28. Ibid., 7.

add, community) "struggles well,"[29] which is implied in Walsh's own understanding of resilience: "the capacity to rebound from adversity strengthened and more resourceful. It is an active process of endurance, self-righting, and growth in response to crisis and challenge."[30]

While some understandings of resilience continue to imply an innate ability to resist the unfavorable impact of extreme stress, more and more attention is falling on the ways that communal (including family) resources assist in undergirding resilience. Research shows that a caring community, both familial and otherwise, is key to building resilience. Werner and Smith highlight several key relational factors they believe positively impacted the resilient nature of the children in Kauai. These include the presence of alternate caregivers, a cohesive sense of family, and "an informal multigenerational network of kin and friends."[31] Likewise, Walsh explores the family as a resource for resilience among its members. She points to three key factors in the family system as being essential to furthering resilience, including: the family belief systems, their organizational patterns, and their communication processes.[32]

Judith Landau and Jack Saul's research on communal response to disaster, including the attack on September 11, suggests that the following are also key resources for developing resilience: building a sense of social cohesion within the community, telling a collective narrative of the community's experience, reestablishing the daily routines and engaging in collective healing rituals, and developing a hopeful vision of the future.[33] We will see at work in the Dinka community some of these very practices, which become significant factors in their remarkable resilience over an extended period suffering.

Meaning Making

At least in part, struggling well in the midst of suffering means finding a way to make some meaning from the experience. Meaning making

29 Psychologist Gina O'Connell Higgins uses the term "struggling well" to describe the adult who not only has endured the deep pain and struggle that accompanies an abusive past but has found strength and healing in the struggles itself so as to move through it into a life of hope (Higgins, *Resilient Adults*, 259–316).

30. Walsh, *Strengthening Family Resilience*, 4.

31. Werner and Smith, *Vulnerable*, 155.

32. Ibid., 26.

33. Landau and Saul, "Facilitating," 304.

happens when we can put suffering and hope in a larger context than the event or experience itself. For the Dinka, as we will see, it requires finding meaning in the context of ongoing violence, uncertainty, and loss. Religion or faith is one of the most significant ways we seek meaning; it is the place we turn when we have exhausted every other effort to answer the haunting question, why?

One of the ways religion and resilience come into conversation is through coping theory. While I do not feel most definitions of *coping* fully grasp the transcendent nature of resilience as I define it, it is certainly an important aspect of the process. Unfortunately, *coping* has no fewer definitions than *resilience*. Kenneth Pargament, a leading researcher in religion and coping, has collected eleven differing definitions of *coping* but chooses this one for his own use: "the search for significance in times of stress."[34] While acknowledging that this search for significance is a process, Pargament does not believe that this search necessarily includes the sacred as an integral aspect. For this he makes a separate category, that of religious coping. Significance is described simply as what is important and can take both helpful and unhelpful forms, which, Pargament notes, is what makes it different from meaning or purpose—both of which are positive.[35] Harold Koenig, a leader in research that attempts to quantify religious experience, also uses the term *religious coping* to describe the coping process that centers on the sacred or religious. He suggests that bringing religious beliefs into the process of coping does not always yield positive coping, which is certainly true. Koenig evaluates the sense of the *positive*, however, by using what he describes as self-reported negative or positive expressions.[36]

On the surface, believing that God is punishing one by means of a particular illness can, indeed, be an unhelpful if not unhealthful theological interpretation. What is missing from Koenig's description, however, is an attempt to understand the context of the situation and what an individual might mean by God's punishment. For example, the Dinka believe, as we will see shortly, that the war was punishment from God. In a time when outside resources were least available, this served

---

34. Additional definitions of coping gleaned from assorted research on the topic can be found in Pargament, *The Psychology of Religion and Coping*, 86. See also ibid., 90.

35. Ibid., 467.

36. Koenig, *Faith and Mental Health*, 46.

to draw them closer together as a family of faith, thus contributing to their survival and ultimate resilience as a community.

In this Christian context, finding meaning, whether we call it an act of religious coping, resistance, or resilience, is one way in which we bring our suffering into the larger frame of God's compassion, love, and restorative justice. This has the power to open the path to hope that despair has covered over.

Summary

We now move toward learning about how the Dinka community has become so resilient during the last decade of war and displacement. As we do so, three ideas are going to be very important to our understanding of pastoral theology and care. First is the idea that an entire community, not just individual members of it, can be a source of care and healing. Second, we are, quite frankly, not accustomed to learning from models of care, pastoral or otherwise, generated from non-Western sources. We are even less prepared to learn from a group of refugees most of whom lack formal education and theological training. Yet they provide a model formed from a very different kind of education that comes from the experience of war and all of the suffering it entails. They also remember something that we sometimes forget about the power of a community bound by a fervent faith to stand resilient in the face of trauma.

Finally, what unfolds in the following chapters tells the story of how resilience within a community is shaped by the context of suffering, the ability to incorporate change, and a faith that helps the people create meaning. Ultimately, as we hear how they negotiate violence and trauma in their own lives, we begin to see possibilities for what we can learn about building resilience in our own circumstances of suffering, violence, or trauma.

2

Ravaged by War

Sudan and the Dinka

[He] described the land in Sudan from which they come. They lived on the Nile so water was always plentiful. Children learned to swim at an early age. Always there was enough water to bathe. They grew gardens for fresh vegetables and gathered fruits and herbs from the forest. They caught fish and killed fresh meat when needed or desired. They raised cattle, though not for food. The land was very fertile. Now this section of the Nile is a feeding ground infested with crocodiles— lured by the taste of human remains dumped by the northern army during the war. Still the crocodiles wait.

—Field notes from Kakuma Refugee Camp, Kenya

NO PHYSICAL, PSYCHOLOGICAL, OR SPIRITUAL EXPERIENCE of suffering can be fully understood outside of its social, cultural, and religious context. Context is likewise essential to framing how an individual or community shows resilience in the face of such suffering. The terrorist attacks in New York City and Washington DC, and Hurricane Katrina, two of the most devastating events in recent American history, help illustrate this point. To say simply that planes flew into the World Trade Center on September 11, 2001, killing nearly three thousand people, does not quite give us insight into the degree of suffering endured or the ways it changed people's view of their place in the world. For example, the perception of national power and invincibility held by most Americans added to the sense of shock and disbelief that it was possible for such an attack to happen on our soil. Even if most people did not personally know anyone in the twin towers, the intimate details of last goodbyes personalized the context through which we came to feel the personal loss of families. Looking at the events of New Orleans during Katrina through the reality of America's long history of slavery, racism, and the fight for civil rights makes us painfully aware of the complex layers of suffering endured by the African American community, abandoned in New Orleans, during Hurricane Katrina. For many, the federal and local political backdrop set a tone of suspicion and incompetence. For both events, 9/11 and Katrina, the political, religious, cultural, and personal contexts deepen our understanding of these extraordinarily traumatic experiences and the resources necessary to navigate them.

Instinctively, the Lost Boys seem to understand this. As I began my work with the young men, I noticed that when asked about their lives, they identified themselves first as Sudanese. Usually, this involved talking about the history of the conflict between the North and the South and about how they were connected to the land. Then they would describe their connection to the Dinka tribe. Finally the Lost Boys would speak most expansively about who they were in what we might call their extended family, or clan. There is no concept similar to our nuclear family. Personal narratives of their experiences during the war were usually framed by participation in the community of Lost Boys. Regardless, their story simply cannot be comprehended in any authentic way without setting the national, tribal, and familial context.

So the objective of this chapter is a simple one: to provide a context that will frame our understanding of the traumatic symptoms and factors of resilience among Lost Boy refugees. To do this will require that we take two paths: first, I will set the political context that has driven the conflict in Sudan, particularly in the last fifty years; second, I will explore the social world into which the Lost Boys were born and to some degree grew up. Together these will allow us to begin to uncover the political, social, and cultural impact wrought by years of war in Southern Sudan.

I will offer a brief overview of Sudan's political-religious history from the early eighteenth century to the present. It's not possible in this limited space to do justice to what is a rich and complex history of a nation. However, even a cursory examination will allow us to identify at least three significant elements, though there certainly may be others, that have progressed over time to create tensions and divisions between the governing regions of the North and the pastoral tribes of the South. They have fueled the conflict in Sudan for generations and add significantly to how the South Sudanese understand their own suffering. First, historically, it is clear that divisions between the North and South are nothing new—even to this century. Rather, they are rooted in a variety of issues that have endured over a substantial period of time and have been used politically to the benefit of many governing parties.

Second, slavery has played a prominent role in politics, the economy, and warfare throughout Sudan's history. Its persistent threat has served to instill fear and resentment in generations of Southern Sudanese, including the Dinka. Over time, slavery can alter deep-set cultural traditions and eventually tear at the social fabric of a tribe or population. Third, famine, from both natural causes and starvation induced as a tactic of war, has also been used politically and strategically to subjugate the southern regions of Sudan. For the government, this has served to physically enfeeble the identified enemy and has in the process weakened Dinka culture by disrupting rituals and traditions in which food holds a primary place. At its worst, famine has caused death and displacement of Dinka families; this in turn further threatens Dinka culture, which holds kinship as primary.

Next I will move more specifically to examine the social world of the Dinka community. I will discuss the importance of kinship, the Dinka relationship to cattle, traditions surrounding food, and certain rites of passage. Exploring the character and held values of the Dinka will give us necessary insight into the Lost Boy refugee community.

What we will find after considering the long conflictual history of Sudan, especially the ingrained divisions between the North and South, the long history of slavery, and the ways that famine has been utilized as a tool of war, is that the Dinka have sustained tremendous loss, not only of life but of cultural heritage. Yet in spite of this loss, they have found adaptive ways to keep certain crucial traditions alive. It is both this loss and resilience that characterize the Lost Boy refugee community.

Sudan

Sudan, a country roughly the size of Europe, is most known for its brutal civil war between the North and South and genocide in the western Darfur region. The last quarter century has been particularly recognized for the hostilities between the northern Islamic National Front government and the Sudan People's Liberation Movement/Army (SPLM/SPLA) in the South. Various sources, the World Press among them, estimate that upward of 2 million men, women, and children have perished since 1983. An additional 4 million have been displaced. Most recently, the world has taken notice of the staggering degree of suffering and death in the western area of Darfur, populated by African Muslims. Estimates range from seventy thousand to three hundred thousand deaths in Darfur from starvation and disease alone in the first six months of 2005. More than 2 million have been displaced. Despite the similar tactics and overwhelmingly high loss of life, the war in the South has never been officially declared to be genocide.

For many of us living in the United States, it is difficult, unless one makes a particular effort, to grasp the depth of the suffering or the issues fueling the Sudanese conflict. Indeed, unless the destruction is significant enough to lure the media and capture the public's attention, Sudan rarely even makes the evening news. When the Southern conflict does emerge as the focus, it is often described as a conflict between the Muslim government in the North and the Christian rebel army in the South, or less precisely, as the Muslims and Christians. To some extent, these descriptions are true. The seat of government is located in Khartoum in the northern region of Sudan with a governing system controlled by Arab Muslims. Islam is the primary religion, Arabic is the language of choice, and Islamic law is enforced. The southern regions of the country, on the other hand, are home to numerous tribes speaking many languages (though most have, over time, learned Arabic as well). Primarily they espouse, practice, and adhere to the Christian religion, although some areas continue to honor traditional African religions.

The issues surrounding this conflict, however, run much deeper than any simplistic dualism (North/South, Muslim/Christian, etc.) reveals. The war in Sudan is fueled by an intricate web of factors, including religion, ethnicity, economics, and politics. It is further complicated by the extreme imbalance of power and resources between the North and South.

Politics and Religion

Ancient history shows an embedded connection between religious, political, and ethnic conviction associated with violent efforts to subjugate the country now known as Sudan on behalf of either Christianity or Islam. We can trace this through a long history of military forces conquering the country. The following table offers a brief sketch of the political and religious influences that have shaped modern Sudan.

Table 2.1: Political History of Sudan[1]

Timeline	Conquering Force	Religious Affiliation	Seat of Gov't. Located	Notable Impact
500 CE	Roman Empire (Justinian)	Christian	North	Coptic Christianity to Nubian tribes in the North[a]
600	Funj (African tribes from the South who advanced northward)	Islam	North	Funj pagan traditions met with Islam through Egyptian political influence in the North. Funj eventually converted and established Islam as official religion.[b]
1800 CE	Ottoman Empire	Islam	North	Cemented Islamic faith in the North; established modern state (monetary system, education, roads, and river transportation); tolerated other religions.[c]
1880s	Mahdist Revolution	Islam (emergence of a savior; rooted in the Shiite tradition)	North	Islamic fundamentalism emerged through this movement.[d]

1. This table is my own creation and is intended to condense a vast amount of information while making it easily accessible to the reader. Dates and events are common knowledge; summary information is my own except where table notes indicate otherwise.

Timeline	Conquering Force	Religious Affiliation	Seat of Gov't. Located	Notable Impact
1899–1955	Britain	North allowed to remain Islamic; missionaries introduced to southern regions	North (Khartoum)	Became a colony of Britain largely to protect interests in Egypt (also a colony)[e]
1955–1958	Sudan gains independence	Islamic	Khartoum	Failed attempts at democracy led to military rule
1960	Sudanese government at war with South Sudan, which continued to resist	Islamic	Khartoum	

Table Notes

a The Nubians were a highly cultured society that occupied much of the northern area of Sudan bordering Egypt and were known for adopting many Egyptian traditions (Walker et al., *A History of the Christian Church*, 179).

b Holy men from Egypt entered the Sudanese territory as teachers and traders (Holt and Daly, *A History of the Sudan*, 26–29.

c Holt and Daly point out that it is not entirely accurate to claim that Sudan was conquered by the Ottoman Empire, though its sovereignty was recognized. Muhammad Ali, viceroy of Egypt in the early nineteenth century, was eager to expand his governing territory and to, perhaps, gain the upper hand over former opponents from Egypt, the Mamluks, who had fled into the central regions of Sudan when Egypt fell to the Turkish. Because of this ambiguity this period in Sudan's history is frequently referred to as the Turco-Egyptian Regime. Also, there is evidence of Catholic missionaries entering the southern regions (Holt and Daly, *A History of the Sudan*, 41–42, 61).

d A charismatic leader named Muhammad Ahmed ʿAbdalla himself claimed to be the Savior (the *Mahdi*) and is described by historians Holt and Daly in this way: "He claimed for himself unique status, reflected in the three titles which he associated with his name – the Imam, the Successor of the Apostle of God, the Expected Mahdi. As Imam, he asserted his headship of the community of true Muslims. As Successor of the Apostle of God, he envisaged himself reenacting the role of the Prophet, by restoring the community which Muhammad had established. As the Expected Mahdi, he was an eschatological figure whose advent foreshadowed the end of the age" (Holt and Daly, *A History of Sudan*, 77).

e British entry onto the scene roughly coincides with the rise of the Mahdi in Sudan. Egypt opened itself to British occupation in 1882 under the auspices of a receivership. While Egypt would go on to gain its independence in 1922, Sudan remained under Condominium rule until 1955.

During the latter part of Sudan's history, the South was not without its own attempts to develop organized government to negotiate on its behalf. From the earliest of times, elders of prominent tribes would negotiate with ruling governors. As early as 1967, a Southern provisional government and a defense army were established.[2] By 1971, the Southern Sudan Liberation Movement (SSLM) was formed and negotiated Southern interests at the Addis Ababa Accord in 1972.[3]

In the 1970s, John Garang and the Sudan People's Liberation Movement and Sudan People's Liberation Army (SPLM/SPLA) emerged as an organized military and political movement that sought a united nation grounded in justice and equality. Dominated by the Dinka tribe, the SPLM/SPLA was not initially accepted by all Southerners. Garang saw the SPLM/SPLA as a national revolutionary force fighting against corruption and violent injustice.

The year 1969 marked the rise of Jaafar Nimeiri, who as a colonel led a bloodless coup and was then elected president of Sudan in 1971.[4] Nimeiri's reign began grounded in diplomacy but ended in religious fanaticism. At the onset, it recognized the differences, cultural and otherwise, between the North and the South. Governors of the three southern regions were even given cabinet positions in Nimeiri's government.[5] The 1972 Addis Ababa Peace Agreement formally recognized these differences and gave limited autonomy to the south, resulting in a brief period of peace. However, this was not to last. Oil was discovered at Bentiu in Southern Sudan in 1978, leading Nimeiri, in a move that violated the country's constitution, to annex the area and to declare it a separate province and himself governor.[6] In 1983, president Nimeiri fueled the escalating hostilities with the south. First, he imposed what are now called the September Laws, that is, the imposition of Shari'a or Islamic law, which dictated severe punishment for crimes, including dismemberment and execution. Second, Nimeiri divided the southern region back into three distinct parts, perhaps attempting to divide the

---

2. Holt and Daly, *A History of the Sudan*, 170.
3. Khalid, *War and Peace in Sudan*, 136.
4. Ibid., 168.
5. Ibid., 136.
6. Ibid., 146–47.

political allegiance in the South. Shortly thereafter, Nimeiri declared himself Imam, the religious leader of the country.[7]

The period between Nimeiri's hopeful beginning and erratic end saw numerous attempted coups, indicating both the weakness of his regime and the precariousness of the politics surrounding it. By the end of his career, Sudan was near ruin. Holt and Daly note, "By 1984–85 the Sudan's economic problems had become insoluble: the urban riots and rural famine that marked the final phase of the Nimeiri era were the inescapable evidence of political as well as economic collapse."[8]

Indeed, corruption had seeped so thoroughly into the governing regime that the road was paved for a military coup, supported by popular consent, which took place in 1985 while Nimeiri was out of the country.[9] A transitional government attempted to maintain this now politically and economically devastated country until the National Islamic Front (NIF) rose to power in 1989.

The NIF's goal was to create a utopian Islamic state that was based purely on Islamic law. This led to the most brutal fighting in the South from 1989 to 1995, resulting in the death and displacement of millions of South Sudanese. Efforts to negotiate peace were ongoing from the late 1990s until 2005, when peace accords were signed by the NIF and the SPLM/SPLA. John Garang DeMabior (more commonly known as John Garang) was appointed president of South Sudan and became one of two national vice presidents. The issue of southern independence was forestalled by six years, after which elections would be held to determine whether the South would remain a part of a unified Sudan.

In the summer of 2005, John Garang died in a helicopter crash on a return trip from Uganda only three weeks after his inauguration as president. Riots broke out throughout the South amid accusations that Garang had been assassinated. Every effort was made to maintain the peace accord, and Garang's lieutenant, Salva Kirr Mayardit, his

7. Daly and Holt, *A History of the Sudan*, 178.

8. Ibid. Mansour Khalid makes a powerful observation about this period saying, "The Nimeiri regime was the most outstanding era in the history of post-independence Sudan . . . [it will] forever stand out as the most wasted opportunity to establish a lasting peace in the South. Rarely had a Sudanese leader since independence had a chance to be a national hero without borders, and thoroughly bungled it" (Khalid, *War and Peace in Sudan*, 133).

9. Khalid, *War and Peace in Sudan*, 159.

right-hand man since the conception of the SPLM/SPLA, was quickly appointed to succeed him. Peace in South Sudan remains tenuous with frequent skirmishes on the North/South border. The first democratic elections, as dictated by the peace accord, were held in the spring of 2010. Bashir was reelected as president amid great controversy over the authenticity of the voting process. In early 2011 South Sudan will return to the polls, this time to vote on what is known as the referendum of self-determination of South Sudan (i.e., independence from North Sudan). While Bashir has publicly announced that he will abide by the vote of the people of South Sudan, the popular belief is that conflict will ensue.

The Problem of North versus South

The differences that separate South and North Sudan are historical and well defined. Geographically, the borders of modern Sudan were not set until the turn of the twentieth century. Until then, definitions of North and South were somewhat obscure. Archeological evidence reveals that the Nubians were known to have settled in the North and extended into what is currently central Sudan. The south, on the other hand, has little such evidence of a single formal social structure but rather is significant for having maintained its ancient history of being inhabited by tribal pastoral peoples who adhered to traditional religious beliefs. In ancient times, this North/South division was further enhanced by a natural barrier called in Arabic the Sudd, a formidable swampland created by the overflow of the Nile during the rainy season that made traversing from North to South nearly impossible (seasonally) until modern times.

The political power of the northern region stems from its geographic location near the heart of ancient Middle Eastern trade routes. Sudan, bordering both Egypt and the Red Sea, has been strategically significant from antiquity to the present day. It is not surprising that empires in control of these trade routes found it necessary to secure Sudan's access by conquering northern Sudan and basing its governing resources in that region.

From the brief sketch of Sudan's history that I have presented, it is easy to see how different one half of the country is from the other in terms of religion, language, and culture. By the mid-twentieth century, the North was firmly rooted in the Muslim religion, and Arabic was the official language. The culture was a mixed one of Arab and African tradition. The south, meanwhile, continued to consider English its official language, though hundreds of tribal languages were also used. The influx of Christian missionaries into the South during the British occupation accounts for a large population of Christianized tribes, though some areas continue to practice traditional African religions. Cultural traditions have continued to reflect those of their African ancestors.

Slavery

Sudan has long been a source for the brutal business of collecting slaves. From the earliest of times, powerful tribes captured members of weaker ones. The ancient Nubian tribes of the North, long before the Turko-Egyptian conquest in 1821, paid homage to the Egyptian rulers by offering slaves captured from surrounding tribes. As the lucrative slave trade hit its stride in the nineteenth century, dominant tribes captured and sold slaves to traders for profit. Further, when the northern areas of Sudan became more populated by Muslims, the territories from which slaves were gathered spilled over into the non-Muslim western and southern regions. Though enslavement of non-Muslim Africans was notable from the ninth century onward, I will focus here on the nineteenth and twentieth centuries.

Under the control of the Ottomans in the nineteenth century, the collection of slaves was particularly insidious. Obtaining black slaves for use in his army and for domestic servants and concubines was one of the primary reasons that Ali, the Ottoman viceroy in Egypt, conquered Sudan in 1821.[10] Interpretation of Islamic law at the time allowed slavery in general but in its original form called for slaves' just treatment and dictated that no Muslim could be enslaved by another.

Slaves were typically taken by one of four methods: war (as prisoners), raiding (gathering of large groups of black slaves from a village or tribe), kidnapping an individual, or purchase.[11] Four areas or groups of people in southern and western Sudan are noted as being the primary focus of the slave trade in the nineteenth century. These include those now known as Equatorians, the Nolithic people (primarily the Dinka and Nuer tribes), a string of weaker tribes living in the plains, and tribes in

10. Savage, *The Human Commodity*, 129.

11. Toledano, *The Ottoman Slave Trade*, 15–18.

what is now the Darfur region.[12] In his history of Sudan, author Mansour Khalid states, "In the South, the brutality with which slave hunting was carried out, and the coarse treatment to which military slaves were subjected, turned the Turkish colonial regime into an object of hate."[13]

The presence of slaves in the Muslim household became fundamental to the Muslim family structure, which is, perhaps, one of the reasons that it took decades to abolish the practice of slavery. Writing about the history of the Ottoman slave trade, Ehud Toledano notes that the seclusion of women and children, the practice for Muslim families, created a need for slaves to maintain the household. He writes, "The harem section housed all the wives, concubines, slave attendants, children of both sexes, and female dependents. The social network of harems all secluded from the male world . . . was an active powerful world unto itself. In it, women ruled over women, maneuvered to manipulate the men's world outside, determined the quality and nature of the upbringing of male offspring, and not infrequently influenced the affairs of state."[14]

It is not insignificant that the maintenance of one social structure came at the overwhelming expense of another. In some cases, especially among the weaker tribes, who by temperament or circumstance were less able to defend themselves, entire tribes were all but driven to extinction.[15]

As trade increased along the Nile, the demand for slaves also increased, beginning an era of what Holt and Daly aptly call "predatory commerce."[16] By 1850, the European market for ivory had increased to the point that the demand could no longer be satisfied through means of trading; this demand fueled vigorous and violent means of collecting ivory by force.[17] The need for slave labor increased proportionately.

The abolitionist sentiments of Britain and Europe in the mid-nineteenth century pushed the slave trade underground. Not until 1891, after nearly fifty years of pressure from Britain, did the Ottoman

---

12. Savage, *The Human Commodity*, 143–47.

13. Khalid, *War and Peace in Sudan*, 4.

14. Toledano, *The Ottoman Slave Trade*, 279–81.

15. Savage, *The Human Commodity*, 144.

16. Holt and Daly, *A History of the Sudan*, 62.

17. Ibid. 61.

Empire legally enforce the manumission of African slaves.[18] Though the practice of taking and owning slaves was not tolerated by the British government during Condominium rule in the beginning of the twentieth century, it is difficult to say that slavery ceased to exist in Sudan during this time. Fear of capture thus marked generations of Africans. Reflecting on the impact of the Turkish slave trade as it ended with the onset of British rule in Sudan, Francis Mading Deng, son of a Dinka chief and prominent scholar on Dinka culture, says, "The Dinka, having just emerged from a world 'spoiled' by the ravaging raids of Arab slavers, had memories to keep and grievances to nurse. As children, we were still frightened into silence by such exclamations as 'there come the camels.' The expectation was that Arabs would capture and put the captives in their large skins on the side of their camels. The foreign ruler did not hesitate to use this for his policies of divide and rule."[19]

Slavery reemerged as a tool of war after independence from British rule. The most notable evidence of this was the abduction of women and children by northern military forces to serve as concubines, domestic servants, and perhaps even soldiers. Robert Collins, writing on the Nilotic slave trade, reports incidents in 1986 among Dinka villages in southern Sudan where as many as seven thousand children and women were kidnapped and sold into slavery by the government forces, a claim the Sudanese government denies. He further notes, "The slaves were used in ways in which slaves have been exploited since time immemorial. The girls and women became concubines, household domestics, and frequently worked the fields."[20]

Refugees arriving in Nashville shared numerous accounts of armies invading their villages and killing all of the adult males while abducting the children and women. Rogue nomadic tribes also threaten refugees with violence and abduction. One refugee, after having arrived in the United States, tells of getting news from relatives that his sister and one of her baby twin daughters had been murdered by just such a tribe. Less

18. Slavery in the Ottoman Empire became illegal in 1897 by governmental decree. However, the illegal status of the slave trade served only to make is a less-public affair. The government failed to consistently enforce the antislavery laws such that it was not until 1891 that slavery was publicly admonished and African slaves set free (Toledano, *The Ottoman Slave Trade*, 124 –47, 246).

19. Deng, *The Dinka of the Sudan*, 137.

20. Collins, "The Nilotic Slave Trade," 158–59.

than a year later, he discovered that the other twin had been sold into slavery and now resides among another tribe in South Sudan. While the "owners" of the child are sympathetic to this family's plight and are willing to return the child, they will do so only at the cost of the original purchase price. This is the ultimate cruelty, to find a missing loved one who has been enslaved and know that the only possibility of returning these children to their families is to purchase them back, and not to have the money to do so. Even refugee camps do not offer a haven from marauding troops in search of human commodity. Sadly enough, the devastation of war and famine have also led some Southerners to sell their own children hoping that they will at least be fed.[21] In perhaps just such a case, while in Kakuma Refugee Camp in Kenya in 2004, I was approached by a teenage refugee asking if I would like to buy his brother.

Famine

The famine that decimated South Sudan in the 1980s cannot be fully explained by natural causes such as drought. Rather, one must also consider the economic and political reasons for sustaining such a famine, especially the benefit reaped by those in power. In other words, there is evidence that the perpetuation of famine has also been used as a tool of war.

In his book *The Benefits of Famine: A Political Economy of Famine and Relief in Southwestern Sudan, 1983–1989*, David Keen proposes that rather than natural forces or even market forces, the *benefits* of famine are the reasons that powerful institutions promote famine and obstruct its relief.[22] What is remarkable about Keen's thesis is that famine is first of all a process—in particular, one that not only causes death and destruction in communities but also creates some benefit to another community with more political power. He goes on to suggest that if famine creates a benefit for a community or institution, it follows that there is reason to obstruct its relief. He offers three reasons that such obstruction might occur, including to force the increase of grain prices, to minimize the unwanted side effects of migration, and to appropriate resources for those who may be less in need but more

21. Ibid., 159.
22. Keen, *The Benefits of Famine*, 5.

politically influential.[23] If famine coincides with a time of war, as is the case in Sudan, it stands to reason that the weakening of enemy forces through starvation would also classify as a "benefit."

For the Dinka, crop failure alone seldom led to starvation within the tribe. South Sudan is a hard and sometimes unforgiving land, but the Dinka had learned over generations how to subsist through a combination of hunting, fishing, gathering wild vegetation, growing crops, and raising cattle. If drought caused a decrease in crop yield and limitation of wild vegetation, they could, at least to some degree, still rely upon hunting and fishing.

As a last resort, they could depend upon their beloved cattle to sustain them. As early as the nineteenth century, however, the Dinka were subject to cattle raids by slave traders or marauding tribal nomads known for their violence. In the early 1980s, hostilities between the North and South escalated, and they once again became subject to raids, this time by northern forces or similar bands of rogue tribes turned militias, who were given free rein in the south. When cattle were stolen or butchered, it not only destroyed a last line of defense against starvation but began to tear at the cultural traditions surrounding Dinka love of cattle. (I will say more about this shortly.)

Even this cursory review of Sudan's history reveals a complex web of factors that have promoted ongoing conflict between the government of Sudan and southern regions of the country, including Dinkaland, as it is known to the Dinka. A long succession of foreign powers has traditionally occupied the North, firmly planting the seat of government in this region, closest to popular trade routes. Consequently, this has laid the groundwork for current political, social, and cultural divisions between the North and South. Natural geographic barriers have further fortified the separation. Governing forces since the time of independence have used these divisions to overtly subjugate the southern tribes. Slavery had a terrible presence throughout Sudan's history and has emerged as a modern tool of war utilized by the government against southern tribes, including the Dinka. Thus, ancient fears of captivity have reawakened in a new generation of Dinka children. Famine has also become a devastating tool of war. Government forces have routinely burned crops and slaughtered cattle. Because of famine's devastating

23. Ibid., 8.

impact, it is in the government's best interest to impede international aid efforts at every opportunity in order to further weaken their so-called enemy. Both slavery and famine have thus left deep scars upon not only the psyche but the social fabric of the Dinka.

The Dinka

Before we can appreciate the damage done to the social traditions of the Dinka, it will be helpful to consider what some of the Dinka rituals and traditions look like in their ideal form. In particular, I will briefly explore social structure, character, and the role of kinship among the Dinka. Next, I will point to ways that the value of food is protected by tradition. Of the characteristics noted among the Dinka, their love of cattle is nothing less than legendary. Keeping in mind what it can mean to lose something valuable in a time of need, I will discuss some of the feelings and traditions surrounding cattle in Dinka society. Finally, as another way of taking in the context of Dinka life, I will discuss child-hood and some of the rituals surrounding rites of passage. Here we can see how kinship, community, food, and cattle enter into the ritu-als, thus further highlighting their significance. We will be able to see how these rituals define and reveal the essence of what it means to be a Dinka. Where possible, I will make note of the ways that the Dinka have adapted traditions to sustain social ties during a time of war.

Social Structure and Kinship

First, let me offer some basic information about the character and so-cial structure of the Dinka people. Dinka Lost Boy refugees take great delight in helping strangers learn the difference between tribes, clans, and subclans. I use the name "Dinka tribe" in the singular form, which Dinka refugees note is acceptable in the United States and often even in Sudan, because so few understand the difference between the tribes. Dinka author Francis Deng, however, notes that there are, in fact, twenty-five Dinka tribes defined by common geographical area, name, and particularities of culture.[24] Within any specific tribe, there are clans defined by a link to a common ancestor that is not always traceable

24. Though Deng notes that basic culture is common throughout all of the tribes, some of the details of how they express traditions are particular to each tribe (Deng, *Tradition and Modernization*, 4).

by bloodline, and subclans in which the defined link is traceable to a particular individual. Within this is the family. The Dinka make great effort to ensure that a woman has no traceable blood relation to her future husband. Dinka households may be polygynous, though usually including only as many wives as a man can afford to provide for appropriately. Conversations with Lost Boy refugees reveal that one or two wives is customary.

By tradition Dinka social order places elder men at the top. Deng uses the term "domination with respect" to describe the relationship between men and women.[25] Women are recognized for their role in bearing a son, who will extend the family name, as well as for their influence upon his character through raising him. In spite of this subservient social position, one can often find influential women elders who have earned great respect among their male counterparts. For some younger Dinka women who have been living in refugee camps during these last ten or so years, the tolerance for domination has diminished with the new knowledge of universal human rights and, in particular, women's rights. Some men are beginning to acknowledge that the successful future of the Dinka and South Sudan as a whole will require a change in attitude toward women's place in society. Progress can already be seen in the intentional increase of girls in local schools and women working outside the home in some larger towns

In temperament, Dinka men can be rather volatile. Fighting is encouraged in youth to strengthen both body and character. In the refugee camps, the Dinka are known to be among the most violent, as demonstrated by the large fights that break out between different Dinka living groups. Interestingly, however, Deng notes, "Dinka never admit to being the aggressors . . . [rather] they exalt themselves as ferocious resisters of aggression."[26]

Yet the context for these behaviors lies in the high value the Dinka place on kinship. By age five, Dinka refugees tell me, a child can name twelve generations of male ancestors. This has been a special source of comfort for a people now scattered across the continents. Continuing the patrilineal line of one's family is the first priority of every Dinka man and wife. To know that a family name will live on through one's

25. Ibid., 9.
26. Deng, *The Dinka of the Sudan*, 6.

son is nothing less than salvation. Deng even uses the term "procreation immortality" to describe the widely held belief that life is continued through one's sons. He says, "Procreation immortality is an extension of this life into the hereafter or of the hereafter into this life through the memory of the dead."[27] This knowledge alone offers comfort to grieving families of those who have died in the war—leaving behind a child, a son, who will take his place in this world.

Most Dinka now profess the Christian faith. But until missionaries began to evangelize in the southern regions of Sudan during the British occupation, most tribes practiced traditional African religions. Regular participation of ancestor spirits was common in the daily life of Dinka, particularly so in rituals of healing. For the Dinka who have stayed in Sudan, it is often acceptable to blend Christian beliefs with ancient ones. For others, Christianity has replaced those rituals and practices, if not the beliefs themselves.

Food

For obvious reasons (with sustaining one's progeny among them), it is not surprising that the production, distribution, and consumption of food are among life's highest priorities in Dinkaland. Food, though, holds more importance than simple sustenance. It represents a connection, an intimacy, within relationship. The Dinka thus have clear expectations for the responsibility and behavior of men and women in the tending of food.

As it is in many cultures, food is an important part of the Dinka creation story. According to Godfrey Liendhardt, an anthropologist known for his work with the Dinka in the mid-twentieth century, the myths of creation vary somewhat across geographic regions but have key identifying features in common.[28] Of particular interest in the version below is the separation between God and woman, and consequently man, because she disobeyed Divinity's instruction regarding food.

> Divinity (and the sky) and men (and the earth) were originally contiguous. . . They were connected by a rope, stretched parallel to the earth and at the reach of a man's outstretched arm above it. By means of this rope men could clamber at will to Divinity.

27. Ibid., 6.

28. Liendhardt, *Divinity and Experience*, 34.

> At this time there was no death. Divinity granted one grain of
> millet a day to the first man and woman, and this satisfied their
> needs. They were forbidden to grow or pound more . . . The first
> human beings, usually called Garang and Abuk, living on the
> earth had to take care when they were doing their planting or
> pounding lest a hoe or a pestle should strike Divinity, but one
> day the woman "because she was greedy" decided to plant (or
> pound) more than the permitted grain of millet. In order to do
> so she took one of the long-handled hoes (or pestles) . . . raising
> [it] to cultivate, she struck Divinity who withdrew, offended, to
> his present great distance from the earth.[29]

For this act, Divinity severs the rope that connects the sky and earth.
As a result, humans will forever have to toil in order to reap food from
the earth, hunger will follow them, and they will be forever subject to
suffering and death.

It is interesting to see how this myth manifests itself in current
traditions regarding Dinka women, farming, and food consumption.
The sharing of food between a husband and wife is an intimate act, and
great ceremony will surround the first meal prepared by a woman for
her new husband. When a bride arrives at her new home, she will do
so with an entourage of female relatives, who will take responsibility
for all of her assigned domestic duties for the first week. She will be
treated much like a guest in her new home. Even once a bride begins
her new household chores, she will not yet prepare the food. After about
a month, a great celebration will take place. A goat will be slaughtered,
and all of the village will come together. The men will butcher the meat
and ready it for the fire while the women bring pots to help with the
cooking. When the meal is ready, the new wife, alone, will serve her
first meal to her husband and his family. This act will be met with great
applause by all who are gathered.

Even with this wonderful celebration, the new wife, out of respect,
will not eat with her husband. Instead she will eat with the other women
and children. Likewise, the men will eat together, sometimes allowing
the young boys to join them. Women will cook, serve, eat, and clean
together. The men will prepare the meat, eat, and join together for long
hours of conversation. Only at the invitation of the husband will the

29. This story's similarity to the Christian story of separation from God is notewor-
thy (Lienhardt, *Divinity and Experience*, 33–34).

wife join him at the table. The Dinka insist that sharing a meal is more than a taboo custom but implies a sense of intimacy reserved only for those who have been married for many, many years. Deng alludes to this intimacy and its power when he writes: "A sanction which the Dinka consider even more serious [than beating] is when a husband abstains from eating the wife's food, usually implying abstinence from her bed."[30]

Cattle

The relationship between the Dinka and their cattle is deep and abiding and far exceeds any similar dynamic in Western culture. Certainly cattle provide for many practical needs (milk, hides for blankets, dung to keep flies away, urine as disinfectant, etc.), and this usefulness alone causes their care to occupy much of Dinka life.[31] While they are not raised in and of themselves for food, they can be sacrificed for special occasions and will be eaten when they die if not contaminated by illness. Ownership and good care of cattle are an indication of a Dinka man's (and family's) dignity.[32] The relationship between the Dinka and cows is explained by an ancient myth described by Deng:

> The Dinka went hunting and killed the mother of the buffalo and the cow. Both, bereft and provoked, vowed to take vengeance against man. The buffalo chose to remain in the forest and attack man whenever he laid eyes on him. (To this day, the buffalo is one of the few animals that will charge against man without provocation.) The cow on the other hand ingeniously preferred to fight man within man's own system: to be domesticated to make man slave for her; to play man off against man; and to cause him to fight and kill for ownership, possession, or protection of her.[33]

This slave-like devotion and deep adoration are described wonderfully in this quotation from a report on livestock for UNICEF's Operation Lifeline Sudan:

30. Deng, *Tradition and Modernization*, 39.
31. Deng, *The Dinka of the Sudan*, 2.
32. Ibid., 17.
33. Ibid., 2.

A Samburu pastoralist from Kenya who has been working among the Dinka for a month said . . . [,] "I thought that we Samburu were experts in cattle keeping. We are the ones who love cattle above all else. But now that I have seen the Dinka I feel that we know nothing about cows. Those Dinka and their beautiful cows . . . when the cows come home in the evening each one has its own rope and its own peg. Each one is examined as it is tied for the night . . .With the Dinka cows . . . each day the place where they sleep is cleaned, with all the dung dried and ready for burning. The fires are lit to keep mosquitoes from the cows so that they sleep well. And then in the morning, the songs begin to the cows. And the cows are rubbed and cleaned all over with the ash of cow dung. The long horns are oiled and shined. I thought we knew about cows but I was wrong."[34]

Cattle are so beloved that they enter into many aspects of Dinka life. They are given as both bridewealth and settlement of grievances. Sometimes as many as two hundred head of cattle will be given for a wife. Cattle are owned by the male head of household and inherited by the male children after they have come of age.[35] Even before the child is old enough to inherit the cow itself, he may claim a particular color pattern and may even add it to his given name.[36]

Childhood and Coming of Age

Children growing up in the Dinka tribe have relative freedom in the younger years. Though they will have chores, the youngest boys and girls (seven and younger) enjoy the opportunity to explore and play. The Dinka are a pastoral people, and much of life centers on caring for the family's cattle. Food is also raised through farming and supplemented by hunting and fishing, all of which are usually tasks that fall to the men of the family.[37] As refugees point out, each person has work in the family. Young boys (eight to twelve) will tend to the calves. Young girls (and the boys to a limited degree) tend to the youngest children. The young girls will be expected to help their mother in the home when necessary.

34. Adolph, *Ethno-Veterinary Knowledge*, 29.

35. Deng, *Tradition and Modernization*, 274.

36. Ibid., 274.

37. The Lost Boys note that women traditionally spend several hours in the day tending to the farming but rarely more. This is, unless a woman is widowed, in which case it will be necessary and acceptable for her to tend to the farming needs.

Boys eight or older may spend a great deal of time helping their father with the farming. As girls get older, some refugees note, they will spend more time helping their mother with duties such as cooking, collecting fruits and berries, fetching water, milking cows, collecting firewood, and tending to the other needs of the family. It is not hard to see the division of labor already reflecting two distinct categories, with child nurturing/household duties falling to the girls and outside production work to the boys.

Cindi Katz offers an interesting insight into how the gender expectations are reflected in the control of space.[38] This comparative analysis explores the traditions of how space is used or controlled during the life transitions of women from a rural Sudanese village and an urban setting in the United States. Katz's premise is that males and females have a relatively similar range of space to which they are allowed access as young children. As a girl grows older, however, this allowable space decreases while boys' increases. For example, girls become more home-bound due not only to household responsibilities but also to what is deemed appropriate social exposure allowed a woman of childbearing years. Meanwhile, as boys mature, they begin to hunt and travel, thus expanding the space and environment in which they are free to move. Katz proposes that the amount of space to which one has access and over which one has control is directly related to the social power that an individual possesses. She notes two especially interesting even if unsurprising observations: "Restrictions upon girls' mobility were rooted in social codes that control access to the female body; and girls' relative lack of experience with environment compared with boys' was a form of de-skilling with enduring implications for them and the society as a whole."[39] This comment may reveal some of Katz's own cultural bias that remaining within the household leads to a diminishment of skill rather than to the enhancement of a different set of skills.

Katz's point seems subtly represented, though, in the crowning event of the celebration ritual for young Dinka girls at the onset of their first menstruation. When a young girl first notices that she has begun to menstruate, according to female Dinka refugees, she will send a friend to fetch her mother. The girl's mother will bring her home and send for

38. Hodgson, *Gendered Modernities*, 173–202.
39. Ibid., 193.

the oldest woman in the village whose firstborn child is still alive. This elder woman will mix together a solution of brick ground into a powder and cow manure that has been baked and also broken down into a powder, then mixed into a paste to be rubbed over the upper body of the girl. The young girl is excused from chores for that day. On the next day a lamb is butchered and cooked. All the girls in the village who are the same age are invited to the feast. The very youngest boys in the village will also be present to represent the wish and prayer that the young girl will have many sons. During the final event in the celebration, the girl will race with her eldest brother to the front entranceway of the home. Whoever wins is, from that point forward, considered eldest and will receive the respect from others that this brings. It strikes me that the race stops at the very threshold of that which will come to define her proper place. While as a youngster she was free to race through the house and around the village, the very moment a young girl becomes eligible for marriage, an invisible barrier binds that freedom.

The coming of age for young men is one of the most important rituals that a Dinka man undergoes. Most of the Dinka tribes initiate boys through a particularly painful ritual somewhere between the ages of twelve and seventeen. The ritual takes place in what would be the fall season for us and is the time just prior to the dry season in Sudan. All of the young men who are of age and have the permission of their fathers gather in a special hut in the middle of the village. Because of the war, today this may only be ten or so boys. Years ago, as many as one hundred boys would undergo initiation together. Their heads are shaved by a very special woman in the village who is qualified because, according to one refugee, she has never lost a child to death. She is considered blessed by God and will represent the mother figure for all of the young initiates.

During this time, which can last as long as a month, the boys will live in this hut and receive special instruction on becoming a man from the oldest man in the village. Each family will bring food to their youngster daily. It is especially important during this time that the boys not touch or be in the company of a female; and that they not touch a cow, its dung, or its milk. This marks a break away from the things of childhood, such as drinking milk and milking the cow (which only women and little boys do). After the period of instruction, there is a prolonged period of celebration in which the boys travel to neighboring villages to celebrate with relatives. Some of these trips can take days by foot. Each journey culminates with a grand feast in which the host relative will sacrifice the finest bull.

For other tribes, initiation leaves literal marks of manhood on the foreheads of the young boys. Deng, who is from the Ngok Dinka tribe, describes the ritual in which all young men of initiation age are gathered for a villagewide celebration. They will spend all their time surrounded by the men of the village. Deng describes the scene in which all the boys lie on the ground while a pit is dug around their heads. Long, deep gashes are cut into the forehead of the initiates as the blood pours into the pit. Boys are not allowed to show any signs of pain or fear. One refugee notes, "In the order of seniority of birth and lineage, the to-be-initiated lie on the ground to receive some seven to ten deep and well-ordered marks across the forehead: the bloodiest and most painful operation in Dinka society . . . The initiates themselves, still and serene, first attempt to chant their boastful words of courage, but soon pass out from excessive bleeding. The initiator turns wild and sometimes stains his face with blood to invoke greater awe. The whole scene is a madhouse. To a stranger, it is madness itself; but to the Dinka it is *dheeng* [beautiful]."[40]

As I reflect on these rites of transition from childhood to adolescence, Cindi Katz's observations seem all the more relevant. Though the rites of passage for both girls and boys are marked by celebration, each represents spatially opposing expectations. For girls, the celebration literally ends at the door of the home and firmly connects her bodily function of menstruation with confinement, the expectation of marriage, and childbirth. The boys, on the other hand, are sequestered communally and expected to travel to regions far from home. Likewise, the initiations of some tribes revolve around withstanding painful experiences in order to separate the emotionality of young boys (which is also associated with women and their caretaking) from the stoic acceptance of the men they have become.

40. One Dinka refugee translates the word *dheeng* as *beautiful* and readily agrees that initiation is a profoundly wonderful moment in the life of the Dinka. So important is this that in spite of volatile circumstances that prevail in Sudan, many of the young men (Lost Boys) desire to return to their villages, at some point, to undergo initiation. One may grow older and even marry, but he will be considered a real man only when the elders of the tribe have initiated him (Deng, *The Dinka of the Sudan*, 70).

Betrothal and Marriage

Courtship and betrothal may begin after a girl has begun to menstruate and a boy has been initiated. Marriage, however, will not take place until the couple is past the age of legal consent in Sudan, sixteen. Traditionally, the Dinka marry by the age of eighteen or nineteen. Adolescent boys and girls are separated during most social activities to ensure that neither gives in to the temptation of sexual indulgence. There seems, however, to be a certain freedom for what we would call group dating (boys and girls of the same age socializing as a group). Some Dinka insist that by the time a young man actually speaks directly to a young woman, he already knows that he wants to marry her. Ideally, it is the girl's choice to marry a young suitor or not. Only if she agrees will the young man approach the girl's father. The parents, in turn, confirm that the girl wishes to marry him. If all agree, the young man gives his betrothed a necklace and/or ring (such adornment is reserved only for those who are married or betrothed) as a sign of their engagement. The groom-to-be is expected to also provide a considerable gift of cattle to the family of his future wife.

The young bride is expected to be a virgin, but at least in modern Dinka tradition, there seem not to be harsh ramifications for indiscretions that do not result in pregnancy. Social pressure and self-restraint are the only methods used to ensure a girl's virginity. On the wedding night, a white sheet is placed on the bridal bed, and representatives from each family wait outside the hut to witness the presence of blood the following morning. If there is no blood, then the bride's family must give two cows to the groom's family, but the marriage remains intact. Young girls are encouraged to be honest with their families prior to the wedding to avoid public embarrassment.

After the wedding, the bride will return to the home of the groom's family, where she will take on the responsibility of tending to the needs of the entire extended family, including the other women. In other words, she must take care of her mother-in-law. One can see how a woman's power begins to increase in the household when her sons marry. If there are several daughters-in-law, duties will be shared among them, often on an alternating schedule so that each has time for needlework and other such pleasant tasks.

The traditions and rituals of the Dinka described here reveal the cultural web that defines the Dinka people. Traditions of food preparation and consumption, so profound in this culture that they enter into myths of creation, help delimit gender roles and bring the community together in times of celebration. Cattle bear a profound influence upon the Dinka and have long been cherished for their practical provisions. So valued are cattle that they play an integral part, both in joining a man and woman in marriage through payment as bridewealth, and in settling issues of justice through payment in bloodwealth. Perhaps the best indicator of the important role cattle play in the life of the Dinka is the fact that characteristics of the cattle are transposed onto the Dinka when they include a color pattern in their actual name. Further, each Dinka rite of passage in some way points to the value of kinship and the celebration of community. The rituals, from childhood through marriage, further define gender roles and prepare both men and women for the task of raising children, particularly sons. With this glimpse of the Dinka social world, we can begin to imagine the impact of the violent circumstances endured by the Lost Boys and other Dinka who have had to flee from their villages, their homeland, and in many instances the very traditions that have defined them for generations.

Summary

In this chapter, I have laid the groundwork for understanding the context from which the Lost Boys of Sudan have come. The long and turbulent history of Sudan reveals a country built on the principles of subjugation. It should be of little surprise to anyone that in its relatively few years of independence, Sudan has not yet found a way to overcome the volatile history that has shaped its existence. Political power has long resided in the northern regions of the country. A consequent imbalance in resources along with cultural, linguistic, and religious differences has driven a wedge between the North and the South.

As we close this chapter, the question is not so much, does the government of Sudan constitute an evil social entity as, rather, how do the subjugating effects of these social entities impact its victims? In some ways, the answers are the same. There seems little doubt that the pattern of violent subjugation by the governing entities, particularly since independence in 1955, has resulted in great loss of life among the southern tribes. Slavery and, most recently, the perpetuation of famine have caused great suffering and added to the rising number of dead. Those who have survived the decades of violence now languish in lands ravaged by war, or in the limbo of refugee camps. A very few have found refuge in distant countries, far from the families and culture that mean so much. This diaspora perpetuates individual suffering that can expand far beyond the borders of Sudan and tears at long-held traditions of tribes like the Dinka.

Examining the cultural traditions of the Dinka has allowed us a glimpse into the world in which the Lost Boy refugees began their childhood before it was so horribly interrupted by war. While we will hear more about their traumatic experiences in the following chapter, here we have at least begun to appreciate the ways war and trauma might impact multiple layers of cultural tradition.

3

The Lost Boy Experience

Kakuma continues to unfold before me. The heat is brutal. Each breeze carries only swirling dust and little relief. All day in the field leaves me covered in dirt and my mouth always dry and thirsty. I hitch rides with UN vehicles but have also learned to travel through the camp as the locals (refugees) do—hiring a Boda-Boda (on the back of a bicycle). Other times I walk. This brings the sense of vulnerability, the grit of the dust and the smells of human waste alive in a vivid way . . . food rations were given yesterday—lines of children and adults whose stomachs have not known food for days. The portions of raw grains are meager but intended to last two weeks. Refugees say it will only last five days. Medicine is limited. Fourteen textbooks must be shared by 120 students. Water is rationed. There is not enough to drink, cook, and bathe. One must choose. The elder refugees seem to have given up hope for themselves and speak only of the children. If they can keep them alive through this horrible time in Kakuma, if they have a chance at education—then Sudan will live. That is their hope.

—Field notes from Kakuma Refugee Camp, Kenya

LOST BOY IS AN IDENTITY BORN OF TRAUMATIC EXPERIENCE. The very name, given by the media, denotes young children who have been exposed to the most brutal realities of war. As we have seen in the previous chapter, Sudan's history of violence and conflict sets the context for what has become known as the flight of the Lost Boys of Sudan.

The story of what happened to these unaccompanied minors is filled with atrocities that most adults have never even considered, let alone experienced. The idea that children could suffer such circumstances seems somehow outside the normal order of things, but in many parts of the world, it is a common occurrence.

The Lost Boys and their plight have received a tremendous amount of media attention—so much that one could almost mistakenly believe that they have suffered more than any other group of children exposed to the atrocities of war. Yet, in the history of war itself, children have always suffered. As I prepare to lay out the context of the Lost Boy experience, I will begin with a brief overview of how some children have been affected by war in the last several hundred years. What will become clear is that the Lost Boys are not unique in their experience of war. Rather, what makes them a significant group in terms of research is how they, as a community, have responded to each other in particular ways that enhance their resilience in the face of incredibly difficult circumstances.

Next, I will frame the story of the Lost Boys around three pivotal periods that emerge from the narratives told by the young men. Though the particular details told by each young man may differ somewhat, there is a remarkable consistency to the overall story that covers more than a decade in the life of these refugees. The first phase is one of war-induced turmoil, during which the children faced frequent threat of death to themselves and those closest to them, were the constant prey of large animals, and were ravaged by disease and starvation. In the end, thousands died. After eventually finding their way to the relative safety of Kakuma Refugee Camp in Kenya, few could have imagined that they would still be living there ten or fifteen years later. This moves us to the second phase of life for the Lost Boys. Even in this refugee camp, life was traumatic enough that it would be wise to consider its long-term effects on the psychosocial health of the Lost Boys. Indeed, as they grew into young men, conflict with indigenous tribes, other Sudanese, or bandits were a constant threat to the Lost Boys. Food shortages, malnutrition, and disease became a way of life, and there was little reason to believe that relief was anywhere on the horizon.

In 2000, efforts by the United States State Department resulted in the resettlement of 3,300 Lost Boys to various cities in the United States. This brings me to the third and final period of transition, which significantly defines the life of a Lost Boy. Living in the United States is different in nearly every way from life in the refugee camp or in their home villages before that. Adjusting to the practicalities of everyday life such as food, transportation, apartment living, weather, and the like was simply overwhelming. The refugees were greatly disappointed to discover upon arrival that they would be expected to work instead of attending school full time, which had been their greatest wish. But even more difficult were the many ways that the individualism so profoundly ingrained in American culture clashed with the deep, abiding connection to community that defines Dinka culture.

These three pivotal periods encompass many emotional, physical, and social struggles that have defined life as a Lost Boy. After considering how these Sudanese children have suffered, we will in the following chapters explore the particular ways the Lost Boys act as a community that has helped them manage the psychological impact of traumatic experience.

Children in War

War affects children. This is a simple reality. They are vulnerable to death, rape, mutilation, disease, and starvation and are even at risk of becoming combatants themselves. A look back over just the last few hundred years exposes an ugly picture of the many ways children become the spoils of war, are used as tools of warfare, or simply become collateral damage.

Written accounts by early settlers in the New England area after the 1637 Pequot Indian War reveal that Indian women and children not killed in the fighting were taken captive by the settlers to be used as household servants. Families were split apart and children sold.[1] Severe punishment awaited adults and children alike who resisted or attempted to flee captivity. Author Michael Fickes notes one young Pequot runaway who reported that "she had been raped and subsequently punished, a branding administered by a local magistrate, for her unwilling involvement."[2]

To consider an example from Europe, wives and children often accompanied Napoleon's soldiers on the long marches during the wars fought for France from 1792 to 1815. Though these families usually

1. Fickes, "'They Could Not Endure That Yoke,'" 59–60.
2. Ibid., 71.

stayed behind the front lines during battle, there was no hiding from the brutal realities of freezing winters, food shortages, or, certainly, injury and death on the battlefield. Over time, male children eventually became incorporated into the units as military apprentices. Historian Thomas Cordoza notes the following:

> Starting in 1786, the French army developed a unique system in which male children were officially incorporated into their parents' regiments as *enfants de troupe* . . . Boys could begin active service as young as two years old . . . Those *enfants* training as craftsmen usually became drummers and buglers, often going into battle long before the age of sixteen. There was strong pressure for this, since drums and bugles provided the only means of signaling on the battlefield and a Napoleonic army would no more go into battle without them than a modern army would go without radios.[3]

A century later, World War II impacted the children of many nations. Most notable, of course, are the children of the Holocaust, who were especially targeted for death because they represented the future of the Jewish people.[4] In addition, thousands of women and girls, many of them Korean, were abducted and forced into sexual slavery by Japanese soldiers. In 1999, the United Nations recommended that the Japanese government accept legal responsibility for the sexual abuse of the "comfort women" during World War II, whose stories are often very similar to this firsthand account:

> One day in June, at the age of 13, I had to prepare lunch for my parents who were working in the field and so I went to the village well to fetch water. A Japanese garrison soldier surprised me there and took me away, so that my parents never knew what had happened to their daughter. I was taken to the police station in a truck, where I was raped by several policemen. When I shouted, they put socks in my mouth and continued to rape me. The head of the police station hit me in my left eye because I was crying. That day I lost my eyesight in the left eye. After 10 days or so, I was taken to the Japanese army garrison barracks in Heysan City. There were around 400 other Korean young girls

---

3. Cardoza, "'These Unfortunate Children,'" 205–7.
4. Sterling, "Rescue and Trauma," 63.

with me and we had to serve over 5,000 Japanese soldiers as sex slaves every day—up to 40 men per day.[5]

On a less ghastly scale, children in London during World War II were separated from families and forced to evacuate with their classmates to the British countryside. Little regard was given to the suitability of foster families, the only criteria being adequate room to host a child.[6] In the United States, far from the battlefields of Europe, children of Japanese descent were herded with their families into internment camps. They were torn from homes, schools, pets, and friends to be confined in the camps. Children looked on helplessly as parents under suspicion were taken away by the FBI without explanation and imprisoned.[7]

Generations of children in Afghanistan, Cambodia, former Soviet bloc countries, and Africa are especially affected by landmines and unexploded ordinances left from current and past conflicts.[8] These "tools" of combat are a particularly insidious aspect of war used with the sole purpose of maiming the enemy. Intended to take adults by surprise, their shape and color are often quite attractive to children, inviting the youngest to literally play with them. Children in rural areas are more frequently injured because farming chores and collecting fire wood place them in the fields and around the perimeters of villages, the very places where mines are likely to be hidden. Margaret Coker, reporting on the war in Chechnya, tells the story of Yusup, a fourteen-year-old boy from a village twenty miles from the Chechen capital, Grozny.[9] After being cooped up in their two-room house during a week of shelling, Yusup's mother gave in to his persistent pleas to play soccer with his friends. Five minutes later she heard the explosion of a Russian cluster bomb that killed seven children and wounded another fourteen, including Yusup. Neighbors helped the mother get Yusup to doctors in a nearby town who told her they lacked the anesthesia and electricity to perform the operation that might save his legs. A new round

5. United Nations Commission on Human Rights, Fifty-Second Session, "Addendum." Online: http://www1.umn.edu/humanrts/commission/country52/53-add1.htm/.

6. Starns and Parsons, *Against Their Will*, 267.

7. Tong, *Race, Culture, and Citizenship*, 12.

8. Machel, *The Impact of War*, 105.

9. Coker, "Tragedy in Chechnya," C7.

of bombing raids kept Yusup and his mother cowered in the basement with the doctors and prevented her from taking him to another hospital. Coker writes, "Gangrene set in to Yusup's shredded legs, forcing doctors sharing the hiding place to amputate them with a kitchen knife, just above the knees."[10]

More recently, children affected by conflicts throughout Africa have drawn the attention of the media. Uganda and Democratic Republic of Congo (DRC) have been of particular concern. In Uganda, groups of children walked as far as ten miles to the nearest town every night just to sleep in a secured area for fear of being kidnapped in the dark of night by the Lord's Resistance Army (LRA). Called the Night Commuters or Night Walkers by the media and aid workers, these children grew to number more than forty thousand. Human Rights Watch estimated that over thirty thousand children have been abducted and forced into combat or enslavement in Uganda since 1986.[11]

Other children have grown up in refugee camps after fleeing war in their countries, some more than a decade ago. For example, Angel was six years old when she was separated from her mother and father as they fled the fighting in Sierra Leone in 1992.[12] Before making it safely to a refugee camp in Guinea, she was held captive for four years by rebel soldiers. While captive, she said, "[The rebels] melted rubber under my feet so that I would not run away"; in the refugee camp, she was raped and became pregnant at age fifteen.[13]

In addition to enslavement, torture, and sexual abuse, children face starvation and disease. UNICEF reports, for example, that only 2 percent of the overall deaths in Uganda in 1980 were caused by some type of violence, while 78 percent of people died from hunger and 20 percent from disease.[14] As chapter 2 noted, starvation is often a tactic of war. At the very least, it is a severe consequence of interruptions in food production due to destruction of crops, inability to plant because of antipersonnel mines, and confiscation or killing of livestock. Distribution of food relief is also interrupted by armed conflict and at times is inten-

10. Ibid.
11. Human Rights Watch, "New Video, New Photo Essay," lines 12–13.
12. Not her real name.
13. Gamanga and de la Guardia, "Childhood," lines 35–36.
14. Ressler et al., *Children in War,* 97.

tionally targeted by opposing forces. Those most affected by decreased caloric intake are growing children.[15]

This brief exploration of children in war reveals that children exposed to military conflict are grossly affected in a number of ways. The Lost Boys are no exception. These stories of children in war show that the Lost Boys are not unique in that they suffered from and fled conflict in their villages or were separated from their parents (though it was unusual to see so many male children together after separation). Many children throughout Africa have suffered and continue to suffer in a similar manner. What is, however, special about the Lost Boys is the manner in which they learned to function within their circumstantial "community" to create systems of care that greatly enhanced their overall resilience.

The Lost Boys

In 1999, 3,300 Sudanese unaccompanied minors and young adults (approximately 3,200 boys and 100 girls), known as the Lost Boys/Girls, were identified by the U.S. State Department as a special refugee population eligible for resettlement in the United States. Among the criteria for being considered for this population was that they arrived in Kakuma Refugee Camp, Kenya, as an unaccompanied minor before January 1, 1995.

Designation as an unaccompanied minor implies that they arrived without parents or other adult family members. This number of 3,300 is greatly reduced from the twenty thousand to forty thousand children who originally fled the upsurge in fighting in the late 1980s to early 1990s. Less than ten thousand children survived the tragic journey, and even fewer have been chosen for resettlement. While there are certainly unique elements of each child's journey, the stories are remarkably similar regarding particular elements. These include the chaos of war and the consequential journey to Ethiopia, the flight from Ethiopia to Kakuma Refugee Camp, and, for some, resettlement in the United States.

15. UNICEF, "The State of the World's Children," lines 3–6.

The Journey

The soldiers came one day when Ajok was, he thinks, six years old. Life since then has never been the same.[16] At the age of six, he was not quite old enough to join his brothers as they tended the cattle outside their home village. One day Ajok, standing near his family's mud hut, heard the sound of planes as they roared overhead and the bombs as they dropped. The gunfire and screams he heard left little doubt that something terrible was happening. Ajok along with others from the village ran until he could no longer hear the gunfire. When he finally stopped, he was lost and separated from his mother and sister.

Terrified, Ajok looked around and saw other boys straggling through the brush. All had the same bewildered, frightened look on their faces. Ajok joined a small group of other boys. He looked for someone he knew and before long found his older cousin Deng.

Deng, who had been tending cattle some distance from the village, also ran when he heard the gunfire, leaving his family's treasured cattle behind. He ran until he could no longer smell the fire that the soldiers had used to burn the huts to the ground. At age twelve, Deng was considered one of the elders in this group of boys.

Deng took special charge over Ajok, carrying him when he grew too tired to walk. The group of young boys and some girls grew in number until there were hundreds, then thousands together. As time wore on, the elder children took over care of the younger children, protecting, disciplining, and encouraging them. These elder children had determined the direction to go was eastward toward Ethiopia, though none knew exactly how to get there or that it was nearly a thousand kilometers away. At each village along the way, they asked directions to ensure that they were on course. Mostly, they traveled at night to avoid the government soldiers and other tribes that might wish to harm them. During the day, they hid in the brush.

At times, wild nuts, berries, and other plants were plentiful; but as the terrain grew more difficult, food became scarce. Often the children had no food or water. There were especially few sources of water as they

16. Ajok and Deng are fictional characters whose story is a composite of many Lost Boys' experience. The information contained in this composite was gleaned from the stories attained from Lost Boy refugees during my time working with Refugee Resettlement at Catholic Charities in Nashville. Where noted, additional information is provided from outside sources.

crossed the desert areas. They were frequently forced to drink their own urine. Ajok recalls eating leaves, grass, and even mud. Author Abraham Nhial, a former Lost Boy himself, describes the harsh land: "Most of the boys were barefoot . . . The rough terrain contained thorns that bloodied their feet . . . 'Some went deep and hurt so bad. They were hard to remove. If we were in a dangerous place, we couldn't stop to take them out even in the daytime.' The boys pulled and cut out the thorns the best they could with other thorns . . . the footprints left a trail of blood on the path behind them—a perfect lure for hungry lions."[17]

Most of the young children came through this experience with stories about the wild animals that constantly preyed upon them. Nhial describes one such encounter with a lion. He writes:

> When the huge animal approached, Yai and the other elders forced the brothers to huddle together in a group with the youngest ones in the middle. At times fright overtook a boy, and he broke out to run despite the elders' attempts to stop him. A lone boy was easy prey to a hungry lion . . . The boys used whatever they could find to protect themselves from the lions. Sometimes the boys succeeded in killing the lion or chasing it away. Too often Abraham watched in horror while a lion dragged away one of his brothers—screaming in pain and begging for help. The cries wrenched at his stomach . . . He didn't want to watch the blood, the gore. After all, he could be the next victim.[18]

Ethiopia

Many months and hundreds of miles later the children crossed the border into Ethiopia. Refugee camps were already overwhelmed by the thousands of refugees, adults and children alike, fleeing the fighting in Sudan. Food was in short supply and many of the already-malnourished children were overcome by the weakness of starvation or diseases such as typhoid, malaria, and dysentery.[19] Gradually, as time passed, conditions improved with the help of increased UN supplies and the creation of an education system in the camps.

17. Nhial and Mills, *Lost Boy No More*, 12.

18. The boys considered themselves brothers to each other (ibid.,15–16).

19. Ibid., 35.

The respite for the unaccompanied children was to end. In 1991, two years after some of the boys arrived, Ethiopia fell into a state of political unrest. Government forces were unsympathetic to the plight of the Sudanese refugees and particularly to the Lost Boys, whom they believed to be rebel soldiers hiding in refugee camps. Ajok recalls the night when soldiers came to their tent. The youngest boys were sleeping in the center of the large tent and were surrounded by the elder boys for protection. Suddenly soldiers appeared and started shooting into the tent. The boys began running and the soldiers pursued them. Eventually the boys came face to face with the Gilo River that separates Ethiopia from Sudan. Without boats to help them cross, the boys were forced to choose between being killed by bullets from the soldiers behind them or running into the river and risking drowning or being eaten alive by crocodiles. Reporter Mark Bixler describes the scene as told by Jacob, one of the Lost Boys:

> The unaccompanied minors had crossed the river several years earlier as they had entered Ethiopia, but its waters had been low and calm then. This time, hundreds of boys lined up along the banks of a river swollen by heavy rain. Crocodiles lurked in the water. Yet Ethiopian fighters with automatic rifles were closing in ... Jacob watched hundreds of boys leap into the river. Some were sucked under by the current, never to surface alive. Others were eaten by crocodiles, the carnage turning the water into a churning red cauldron of parts of bodies and scraps of clothing.[20]

Those who survived the river crossing found themselves again facing a long and dangerous journey to an uncertain destination. The nongovernmental organizations (NGOs) in Sudan and surrounding countries were aware of their plight and provided food drops when breaks in fighting allowed. They had begun to call the children the Lost Boys. Some of the boys attempted to find their way back to their home villages in the hope that even after several years they could locate family members. Some joined the rebel army. Others headed for another refugee camp just fifty kilometers south of the Sudanese border, in the northern regions of Kenya, called Kakuma.

20. Bixler, *The Lost Boys of Sudan*, 10.

Kakuma

Firsthand accounts of the long internment in Kakuma Refugee Camp make it clear that traumatic circumstances did not end for the Lost Boys when they arrived at the camp. Kakuma was built in the semiarid land of northern Kenya, historically inhabited by a tribe of nomadic pastoralists, the Turkana. Temperatures during the day generally stay above 100 degrees Fahrenheit (40 C) and dip only into the upper eighties at night. Fierce winds keep clouds of fine dust moving throughout the camp during the day, obscuring vision and making even simple chores more difficult. A thin veil of grit covers everything. During the rainy season (October and November), two seasonal rivers that surround Kakuma, the Taracich and the Nakabet, flood, putting refugees housed nearby at risk of being swept away in the raging waters.[21]

The camp was created in 1992 to aid thirty thousand refugees, mostly Sudanese, who spilled across the borders. Within a few years, however, it had come to accommodate refugees from at least six other nations.[22] By 2003, when I visited Kakuma, its size had expanded threefold, and the number of refugees housed there had grown to over eighty thousand. Indeed, life at Kakuma Refugee Camp, run by the United Nations High Commissioner for Refugees (UNHCR), has always been difficult and brought continued threat to the unaccompanied minors due to shortages of food, lack of security, and health issues. Abraham Nhial describes Kakuma in this way:

> The camp grew to mammoth proportions. With expansion came conflicts arising from different cultures, religions, languages, and the overwhelming needs of so many people separated from their homes and forced to live in cramped quarters. Violence frequently erupted. Lack of proper sanitation and shortages of medicine ushered in disease. Surrounding villages would raid the refugee camp for supplies. For the Lost Boys, their life spun with turmoil. Kakuma existed as a safer place than Sudan and Ethiopia, but they still lived in fear and instability. They had no

21. IRIN, "KENYA," lines 3–10.

22. In addition to Sudan, other countries represented include Ethiopia, Uganda, Rwanda, Burundi, Democratic Republic of Congo, and Somalia (Berhane-Selassie and Berhane-Selassie, "An Evaluation," 13).

other place to go, and no guarantee any other location would
be better.[23]

It is the custom of the UNHCR to allow the governing council of elders within each cultural community to determine the placement of
newly arriving refugees. In other words, tribes and clans do everything
possible to make room for their own within the same area of Kakuma.
Directly after arriving at the camp, the Lost Boys were placed in living
groups of four or five.[24] They were instructed in the building of living
huts made of dried earth that would become their homes. These groups
of boys were placed together in compounds that included maybe four
or six huts each. Select male elders were paid incentives to look over
the groups and provide cultural education and discipline for the young
boys.[25] Meanwhile, girls who arrived with the boys, having navigated
the same hardships of this long journey, were placed individually into
foster households (nonblood kin) willing to provide care for them.[26]
This will be discussed at greater length later in the chapter.

Food and Water

For ten or more years, the Lost Boys, along with other refugees, lived
with only a minimal amount of food provided by the UNHCR. It is
important to note that food in all refugee camps run by the UNHCR is
donated by a long list of countries the amount of which, unfortunately,
fluctuates from year to year. For example, a UNHCR report noted that
there was a severe global reduction in food donations between 1992

23. Nhial and Mills, *Lost Boy No More*, 75.

24. This form of group living is somewhat familiar for Dinka boys. In a traditional
Dinka upbringing it is customary for preadolescent males (and sometimes females) to
leave home for short periods of time to live in cattle camps where they are responsible
for tending the family cattle. In the cattle camps they primarily cared for themselves
(Derib, *Group Care*, 5).

25. Incentives are minimal amounts of money paid monthly to refugees by NGOs
for a variety of services rendered by the refugees. Since refugees are not legally able to
work in Kenya, according to rules set by the Kenyan government, this small token serves
as a salary of sorts (Berhane-Selassie and Berhane-Selassie, "An Evaluation," 44).

26. Though very culturally appropriate to Dinka beliefs, this proved to be a detri-
ment to the possibility that these young girls would be resettled individually in the
same manner as the Lost Boys.

and 1996, the beginning years of the Kakuma camp, decreasing food aid by nearly one half, from a total of 15.4 metric tons to 7.6 metric tons.[27]

The Lutheran World Federation (LWF) in conjunction with the World Food Program (WFP), on behalf of the UNHCR, is charged with providing for the basic needs of the refugees at Kakuma. These include services to provide food, water, sanitation, and shelter.

Table 3.1: 2001 Basic Food Provisions per Person per Day Distributed Every Fifteen Days

Daily food ration	Ration in grams/ kilograms	Amount in pounds/ ounces	Used in trade for milling/fuel/other	Remaining ration
Raw maize	235g	.52lb	25g (milling) 16.5g (fuel) 16.5g (other)	.39lb (177g)
Wheat flour	220g	.49lb	16.5g (fuel) 16.5g (other)	.41lb (187.5g)
Corn/soy blend	60g	.13lb	n/a	.13lb
Salt	6g	.21oz	n/a	.42 Tablespoon
Oil	25g	.88oz	n/a	1.76 Tablespoons
Wood	.33kg (10kg/mo)	.73lb	n/a	.73lb

* Ration amounts and trade percentages denote estimates from 1999 to 2001.[28]

According to a report from the country director for the International Rescue Committee in Kenya, "the minimum caloric requirement for one person for one day is 2,100 kilocalories"; but the average twice monthly ration in 2001 equated to only 1,770 kilocalories or less (with three months of food shortages that reduced ration distribution to only one per month).[29] It is significant to also note that the rations in and

27. United Nations High Commissioner for Refugees, *Refugee Children and Adolescents*, para. 106.

28. This is my own table with information from Berhane-Selassie and Berhane-Selassie, "An Evaluation," 39.

29. Daily food rations are noted in this 2001 report to the Senate subcommittee (United States Senate, *Testimony,* 1). Figures for the wood rations and estimates of food traded in exchange for fuel, milling, other foods, and other necessities are taken from the 1999 Food Economy Report by Save the Children Fund. (The term *kilocalorie* is the

of themselves do not accurately represent actual food consumed by the refugees. As the above chart indicates, food, often the only viable resource available to the refugees, is frequently traded for things such as the service of grinding the maize to make it suitable for consumption, for medicine, clothing, firewood, and other necessary commodities. This leaves the refugees with considerably less than the minimum caloric requirement. Lost Boys resettled in Nashville frequently told us that they had only one meal a day, which was always eaten in the evening. Aside from the practical point that food cooked during the midday would be filled with the dust that moves through the camp, they said that the day is too long if one does not have food to look forward to at its end.

Various programs throughout the camp attempt to supplement these low food rations for the most vulnerable refugees, who include children under five, pregnant and lactating women, and those with HIV/AIDS.[30] The educational programs also provide additional sustenance such as a corn/soy blend in the form of porridge during the school day for children who are in attendance.[31]

One of the coping strategies used by the refugees to combat these food shortages is the obtainment of ration cards no longer used by refugees who have left the camp for some reason.[32] The rations from these cards become "money" with which a refugee can trade for meat, wood, water, medicine, or other necessities. The additional resource is so important to the sustenance of the refugees and the overall economy of the camp that yearly censuses required by the UNHCR are met by violent resistance. These censuses are intended to adjust food rations in accordance with the actual number of refugees living in the camp.

---

equivalent of what we call a calorie. (Save the Children Fund in the United Kingdom, "Save the Children Fund: Kenya Refugee Study," 16).

30. Save the Children Fund in the United Kingdom, "Save the Children Fund: Kenya Refugee Study," 1.

31. Ibid., 26.

32. Though the Kenyan government stipulates that refugees are not allowed outside the camp grounds without the explicit permission of the UNHCR, refugees frequently move between Kakuma and Nairobi. Many Lost Boy refugees now living in Nashville have noted that the conditions are often so bad in Kakuma that they choose to take their chances living in Nairobi. When a refugee leaves the camp he or she often leaves his or her ration card with a family member or friend so that they can receive additional food.

Indeed, such uprisings can and have successfully delayed the census taking by months at a time.

Other sources of income are limited for refugees. The UN and other NGOs hire refugees for certain jobs with great regularity. Since they are not allowed by the Kenyan government to work for salary, and to avoid the appearance of NGOs' fostering a relationship of dependency, they receive what is called *incentive pay*. This is well below standard pay but can average around 33 $US/month, making incentive employees among the wealthiest in the camp.[33] Some refugees arrive with money from businesses they left behind. This is particularly so of the Somali population, who have become among the most notable merchants and traders in Kakuma. Others receive money, called remittances, from relatives living and working in countries outside Kenya, especially the United States. Clearly, in spite of the sparse circumstances of life in Kakuma, there is a thriving economy that results in the creation of socio-economic classes among the refugees.[34]

As of 1999, Kakuma's water system included six boreholes that distributed water through only 472 taps intended to serve the entire population of over eighty thousand refugees.[35] The taps are opened twice daily for the collection of water. When refugees arrive at Kakuma, they are given a minimum number of containers for the collection and storage of water based upon the number of persons in the family. Over time, families will salvage or purchase, as is possible, additional plastic containers for water storage. Long before the appointed hour, refugees, mostly women, will begin to stand in line with as many containers as they have to collect and then carry the water to their huts. Though this water system is intended to provide the minimum international standard of 15–20 liters per person per day for all sections of the camp, some areas have at times had access to only less than 5 liters per person per day.[36]

33. Save the Children Fund in the United Kingdom, "Save the Children Fund: Kenya Refugee Study," 20; Lawrence et al., "Household Food Economy," 20.

34. As much as 40 percent of the Kakuma population in 1996 was considered to be among the *poor* or *poorest* in the camp, whose major source of income was from the sale of rations. Socioeconomic categories include Rich (1–5 percent), Middle Incentive (35–45 percent), Less Poor (15–25 percent), Poor (25–30 percent), Poorest (10 percent). (Save the Children Fund in the United Kingdom, "Save the Children Fund: Kenya Refugee Study," 21).

35. ACT International, "Appeal", 8.

36. United States Senate, *Testimony*, 4.

The food and water shortages, consistent throughout Kakuma's history, increase risk to refugees in several ways. Most obviously, it puts the most vulnerable refugees (children, pregnant and nursing women, the sick and the elderly) at greater risk for disease and death. It also increases the potential for violence among refugees, who, out of desperation, turn to theft and banditry among neighbors to meet their needs. This violence is further perpetuated through conflict with the local Turkana tribe when refugees are forced into the areas surrounding the camp in search of food and other resources.[37]

Physical and Emotional Illness

Malnutrition is one of the leading underlying causes of disease among refugees at Kakuma. The gross lack of variety in available food choices, especially those rich in vitamins A, B2, C, and B3, have resulted in an overwhelming prevalence of anemia among the refugees.[38] Poor sanitation has led over the years to various outbreaks of cholera; malaria is of constant concern, while diarrhea and respiratory infection continually plague children of all ages. The International Organization for Migration (IOM) requires HIV/AIDS tests for all refugees who are under consideration for resettlement. (Some countries, including Canada and Australia, will not accept HIV-positive refugees for resettlement.) This information, however, is not released to the other NGOs in the camp, so estimated infection rates of 7 percent cannot be substantiated. Accurate death rates are unavailable largely due to the overall lack of resources in the refugee camp.[39]

Upon meeting refugees resettled in Nashville, it is quickly apparent that refugees are well versed in the causes and symptoms of PTSD as proposed by Western diagnostic measures (such as the DSM-III or IV). Indeed, refugees in Kakuma are frequently diagnosed with PTSD. I will discuss this in greater detail in a moment. Other psychosocial issues such as depression or mental illness are addressed by a team of lay counselors who are trained to administer regulated doses of select drugs such as antipsychotics. This team is overseen by the one psychiatrist

37. Ibid., 4–5.

38. Lawrence et al., "Household Food Economy," 2.

39. From interviews I conducted at the refugee camp, I learned that infection rates for Lodiwar are stated to be as high as 18 percent.

employed by the International Rescue Committee (IRC), which provides medical care in the camp.

Threat of Violence

Though life in Kakuma is certainly safer than a war zone, Kakuma is a violent place. Security is compromised by several factors. Among these is the conflict among the Sudanese tribes that can be further exacerbated by the close living space and difficult conditions. Another source of violence stems from the infiltration of various persons or groups into the camp. For example, factions from the rebel army, bandits, or those seeking to abduct women or children are a common concern at Kakuma. Perhaps the most extensive and consistent conflict occurs, however, between the refugees and the indigenous tribe, the Turkana, who live on the land surrounding Kakuma.

The land upon which Kakuma was built is located in the Turkana district of northern Kenya, which continues to be home to the Turkana tribe. The Turkana have a distinct appearance: the women wear beaded neck rings that when stacked one upon the other, over time, stretch the neck. This gives them a tall and regal stature, though they seldom smile or offer a gesture of welcome to strangers. Their clothes are of bright material woven and designed in a likewise distinctive way. Raising cattle remains their primary source of wealth and sustenance in this region where life is difficult even when weather and other factors are at their best.

During difficult times, such as drought, the Turkana have traditionally received little help from the Kenyan government. It should not be a surprise, then, that hostile feelings arise when Turkana land is taken without compensation to house, feed, and provide aid to refugees. The Turkana claim that the refugee presence is detrimental to the Turkana in a number of ways, including through the introduction of diseases such as HIV/AIDS; through the environmental impact, including the disappearance of indigenous vegetation; and through the increased shortage of water.[40] The LWF notes that "since the refugees have been supported by the UNHCR and their various implementing partners[,] . . . the Turkana expected that they would get similar support and access to services and benefits such as food, water, health, shelter and other

40. Berhane-Selassie and Berhane-Selassie, "An Evaluation," 18.

community service assistance, (just like the refugees) in return for playing host to the refugee community."[41] Not until 1999, when severe drought decimated Turkana cattle herds, did the LWF engage in relief efforts. Through the Turkana Emergency Relief Project (TERP), water services were provided to the Turkana. According to a 2001 evaluation of the Kakuma Refugee Assistance Project, continued services of this sort have also become important to "refugee peace and wellbeing."[42]

The Turkana have otherwise compensated for the shortage of necessary goods by, some refugees claim, using violence to influence camp economy in their favor. For example, as previously noted, the refugees are provided with 10 kg of firewood by the UNHCR each month. This leaves the refugees dependent upon the land surrounding the camp to supplement what is a considerable shortage in their fuel supply. By subjecting women, who traditionally tend to the chore of wood collection, to rape and other forms of violence when they leave the camp to gather wood, *then* collecting the wood themselves to sell to the refugees, the Turkana have created a market niche that provides them with a feasible income.

Though living in nearby villages, the Turkana are free to move throughout the camp. NGOs in the camp adhere to a strict 6pm curfew after which all aid workers must return to compounds with perimeters marked by barbed-wire fencing; some compounds are further protected by patrolling guards. The refugees, meanwhile, live in huts mostly without secure doors within living compounds protected only by the thorny branches woven into makeshift fences that mark a family's living space. Many raids and personal assaults on refugees that occur during the night are blamed on the Turkana.

Large-scale fighting that hardly can be blamed solely on the Turkana often breaks out with the refugees. Such skirmishes often quickly escalate, leading to death for some and internal displacement and interruption of services for thousands. In June of 2003, it was reported that an uprising over cattle rustling resulted in the deaths of ten refugees and two Turkana (from gunfire) and in the displacement of up to thirty thousand refugees. It is important to note that this violence is not just random behavior but a cultural rivalry between two groups

41. "The Forgotten People of Turkana," in Lutheran World Service/Department of World Service, *Annual Report*.

42. Berhane-Selassie and Berhane-Selassie, "An Evaluation," 17.

that have, as UNHCR official, Cosmas Chanda says, "similar value systems."[43] Integrated Regional Information Networks (IRIN) News goes on to note: "For both the Sudanese Dinka and the Turkana, cattle ownership is a way of life, a means of trading and paying dowries, and a manifestation of a person's worth. The Turkana have managed to maintain a traditional lifestyle assisted greatly by the proliferation of arms in this largely unpoliced part of Kenya in which cattle-rustling plays an important role. 'For a man to be recognized in society, he needs to be able to raid [cattle],' says Chanda. But while the Dinka of South Sudan have similar values, they are forbidden from keeping cattle in Kakuma camp—to which they are confined—which has eroded both their material wealth and their sense of identity and worth."[44] But frequent fights also break out between groups of refugees. The Dinka in particular are known by aid workers to be among the most violent of the refugee groups. Dinka will easily engage Dinka or refugees from other tribes in fights. At times, entire sections of the camp must be secured by armed reinforcements called in to restore order.

Camp Resources: Religious and Educational

The refugees can themselves be credited with the construction and administration of the many churches found in Kakuma. The fact that no assistance for these needs has been provided by NGOs that are themselves church based is frustrating and bewildering to most refugees.[45] Education is provided by NGOs other than LWF. The LWF is only responsible for basic needs. At different points throughout Kakuma's fourteen-year history, in spite of the hardships encountered there, it was the only place that the Sudanese could obtain an education. Many refugees are rumored to have abandoned the Sudanese rebel army and fled to Kakuma to go to school.

The Lost Girls

I will take just a moment to discuss the young girls who traveled with the Lost Boys on the long journey from their villages to Ethiopia and,

43. IRIN, Marginalised Turkana.
44. Ibid.
45. Berhane-Selassie and Berhane-Selassie, "An Evaluation," 21.

finally, to Kakuma. They have become known as the Lost Girls. Due largely to cultural tradition but aided by UNHCR policy, they have met a very different fate from the majority of Lost Boys.

Based on cultural tradition intended to protect girls within the family structure, most of the unaccompanied girls were placed into foster households.[46] The details of how this transpired become very important to the overall picture of the question asked frequently since the resettlement of the Lost Boys; that is, what happened to the Lost Girls?

When a girl is placed into a nonkin household, her individual identity, in a sense, becomes subsumed into that of the family. She is, in most cases, no longer listed as an individual refugee, eligible for a food-ration card and the independent status necessary for resettlement. Usually, the foster household's family size is increased in the camp records, which allows for a subsequent increase in family rations. In some cases, however, even this is overlooked, thus placing the child in the vulnerable position of taking from a family's already-scarce food supply. Why would any family already suffering under difficult circumstances take on the added responsibility of another child? There is little question that the Dinka community feels a cultural obligation to provide for children who are lost or separated from parents and extended family. In most cases, there is little reason to believe that these children will be treated any differently from other children in the household.[47] However, we cannot entirely dismiss other motivations. For example, a female child can be seen as an investment in a family's future wealth. When a father feels his daughter, even a foster daughter, has reached an age of marriage, he can demand a substantial bridewealth for the family. The Kakuma Evaluation Report notes the following:

> The lack of interest in the details of their [women's/girls'] lives
> has led to the failure of differentiating refugees as merely . . .

---

46. According to Save the Children in Sweden, who were responsible for the oversight of at least a large portion these Sudanese foster households (which they call attachment arrangements), "in normal circumstances children are the responsibility of parents, extended family members, clan members/leaders and the community at large. Fostering within these social networks is a normal practice, though care within the extended family is always the preferred choice, and there is a moral obligation to provide care for children who lose one or both parents. Fostering is transformed into adoption when the issue of dowry, compensation payment and inheritance come into play" (Derib, "Group Care," 4).

47. Ibid., 13.

men, women, and children. While differentiation according to the causes of fleeing their homes has led to resettlement as a solution to the problem of the so-called Lost Boys among the youth in the camp, its gender blindness has led to the invisibility of the girls from the same background who are reportedly absorbed into the refugee community . . . The invisibility of the girls has led to the prevalence of their early marriage, ghost marriage or abductions while in foster care in the camp![48]

So, while the unaccompanied boys retained their individual refugee status, the girls were subsumed into a family and would be able to seek resettlement only with that family. Eventually, this caused many of the girls to lose the option of future resettlement as part of the unaccompanied-minor program that brought the Lost Boys to the United States in 2000.

The Lost Boys Resettle in the United States

In 2000 the Lost Boys were identified by the US State Department as a *special population* eligible for resettlement in the United States. A *special population* denotes individuals for whom specific elements of their displacement put them at greater risk even while in a country of refuge. The number of refugees resettled as a special population is in addition to the number of refugees allowed into the United States, a number set annually by the president. Mike O'Keefe was the Refugee Assistance Officer for the Horn of Africa when he met the Lost Boys in 1997 and championed their cause with the State Department and NGOs, both of which were concerned about moving young men and children so far away from their own culture.[49]

The number of Lost Boys in Kakuma at the beginning of this process in 1997 is difficult to estimate because of the fluid movement of refugees out of the camp. (Though leaving the camp is technically against the rules, such movement is very hard to enforce.) It is also difficult to distinguish between those unaccompanied minors who arrived before 1995 and the influx of those arriving much later but anxious for an opportunity to attend school in the camp. By 1997, some estimates place the number of Lost Boys at less than ten thousand. Of those who met

---

48. Berhane-Selassie and Berhane-Selassie, "An Evaluation," 13.

49. Bixler, *The Lost Boys of Sudan*, 81–84.

the criteria determined by the State Department (having arrived before 1995, not living with parents), 3,400 were approved for resettlement in the United States. Of these, only approximately 15 percent were still minors under the age of eighteen. This program has certainly benefited the refugees resettled through it, but it has also left behind hundreds (perhaps thousands) of young adult Sudanese Dinka refugees who cling to the identity of being a Lost Boy in the hopes that it will be their path out of Kakuma.

Before leaving for the United States, the Lost Boys took training classes provided by agencies at Kakuma to help orient them to some of the customs and culture of America. These included particularities such as flush toilets; electricity; and expectations of work, food, safety, medical care, and the like. Nothing, however, could adequately prepare these young men for the life they would discover in the United States. Abraham Nhial describes it this way: "Where once there was a sea of ebony faces, there's now a mixture of Caucasian, Latino, Asian, and a whole range of brown to black skin. Apartment living is a challenge to the senses: the sound of a flushing toilet or the hum of a refrigerator, the sight of gadgets in a modern kitchen, the tastes and smells of unusual foods, the touch of a solid wall instead of a tent or rough shelter, and the softness of carpet underfoot."[50] This is a poignant testimony to the way that cultural change of this magnitude can literally overwhelm the senses of a newly arrived refugee.

The refugee-resettlement agencies focus on the most pressing adjustments concerning the practical elements such as food, electricity, apartment living, transportation, and work. Some of the things we take for granted are quite startling to refugees, who have never before lived in a city. The Lost Boys had difficulty judging the distance between steps as they ascended or descended stairs. There are no buildings with two floors in their villages or in Kakuma. Living with electric lights and all manner of electronic devices available in this country is quite contrary to life in Kakuma, where electricity is generator driven and usually reserved for the UNHCR and NGOs. The abundance of food is shocking, the taste of most packaged food is too sweet, and even familiar foods such as chicken or beef carry a foul taste (most likely the result of antibiotics and chemicals fed to the animals before slaughter).

50. Nhial and Mills, *Lost Boy No More*, 142.

Most of the young men arrived wishing to attend school full time. The desire for an education is a common longing for Lost Boys, who dream of one day returning to help rebuild Sudan. All were extremely disappointed to learn that they would be expected to work full time and attend school only in their spare time. Many were also greatly disappointed that their Kakuma education did not leave them adequately prepared for even a high-school level here in the States.

Perhaps the most difficult adjustment of all has been to live a life of abundance while their families struggle every day simply to stay alive in Kakuma or Sudan. The Lost Boys are deeply mindful of their commitment and obligation to provide for their loved ones. Well-meaning resettlement workers and volunteers repeatedly chastise refugees for sending large sums of money to family in Kakuma. Yet the Lost Boys are committed to those they have left behind. This shapes the quintessential struggle between the rampant individualism of American culture, which tells them to save their money for themselves, and the communal obligation into which they were born as Dinka, which says one cannot have what the others do not.

Summary

I began this chapter by stating that the Lost Boy identity is one born of traumatic experience. Indeed, the story of their escape from the fighting that destroyed their villages bears out this claim. Through each phase of their story, the chaos, the journey to Ethiopia and finally to Kakuma, the boys faced constant threat of death from soldiers, wild animals, starvation, and disease. So pervasive was this threat that perhaps as many as thirty thousand children died. Those who survived long enough to reach Kakuma Refugee Camp found not a safe place of rest but the continued threat of violence and severe lack of food (and at times water) along with the continued threat of disease. The Lost Girls became doubly lost as they were subsumed into foster families, often surrendering any chance for individual resettlement. The final phase of the Lost Boy journey was their move to the United States. Few would argue that life was indeed better. But adjustments to this new culture bring a different kind of threat, particularly to the cultural commitments to community that sustained them through the worst of times. It is this community that marks the uniqueness of the Lost Boy story. Like children throughout history, the Lost Boys have suffered in numerous ways because of war. But it is how they function as the community of Lost Boys that has served them in particular ways to help overcome the psychological impact of the trauma they have endured.

4

Refugees and the Effects of Traumatic Experience

I met today with Mr. C, a Sudanese man, who directs the mental health clinics in the camp (Kakuma, 80,000 refugees). He seems to have little formal training in terms of higher education but has been involved in the program for several years. He took me on a tour of two of the centers, each of which is staffed with 3 to 5 counselors depending on R&R rotations. Estimates are that they see upwards of 600 patients per month. These patients come to the clinic for medications and counseling. When asked, the counselors do not seem to have any particular model of therapy or theory upon which their counseling is based. They work with families to help educate them about mental illness and how to care for the individual. Each afternoon the counselors make home visits to follow up on patients who need more intensive home care. Dr. W is the only psychiatrist assigned to the camp, and he oversees this mental health program. I was surprised to learn the counselors also prescribe medications. The team of counselors receives some initial training and then four or so in-service trainings per year from psychiatrists and psychologists who come to the camp. According to Mr. C, lists of symptoms are matched with strict protocols in order to determine if medication is required. Dosage is determined by protocol only. The narrow list of medications available to them includes: For psychosis—Largactil @ 200mg and/or Artane at 5 mg, for epilepsy—Phenobarbital @ 100 mg or Tegretol at 100mg, and for anxiety disorders and depression—Loroxyl at 25mg. Epilepsy, he said, has been very pronounced in the Sudanese community. It is treated as a psychological issue for those whose illness has resulted in brain damage that manifests itself in psychological dysfunction. When asked about the ways in which cultural beliefs conflict with the Western models of therapy, the counselors admitted to understanding these conflicts; but it did not change the course of treatment.

—Field notes from Kakuma Refugee Camp, Kenya

IN WESTERN CULTURE, TRAUMA HAS BECOME SYNONYMOUS with posttraumatic stress disorder (PTSD). Since September 11 and Hurricane Katrina, PTSD has become a part of the vernacular in the United States. Everyone from the local newscaster to the average person on the street can be heard speaking of trauma. Derrick Summerfield, lecturer at the Institute of Psychiatry in London, notes that while most people shy quickly away from other psychological diagnoses, PTSD is a very popular one to have.[1] This has become true, to some degree, also for refugees for whom mental health care became a priority in the early 1980s. What exactly is PTSD?

This chapter examines PTSD and its various applications as well as critiques of its use in refugee populations. The topic of PTSD is broad, so I will be focusing on the application of PTSD in refugee populations. Because PTSD is a psychological diagnosis, this discussion will necessarily be technical and filled with the jargon of mental health assessment, diagnosis, and treatment. But this in itself helps describe the nature of Western psychological paradigms. The details of its inner workings are not intended for the layperson but for the highly trained professional. Nonetheless, it will be helpful to explore the ways Western diagnoses, assessments, and treatments have (or have not) been adapted to suit the cultural needs of refugees around the world. Let me state from the outset that I have no desire or intention to attempt to prove or disprove PTSD as a valid diagnosis, either in the Western context or in refugee populations. I do confess, however, that I carry a bias toward caution when PTSD diagnosis and standard treatment protocols are applied transculturally. As I said above, the unqualified and universal application of PTSD diagnosis and treatment to refugee populations can distort "symptoms" and overlook valuable sources of resilience. To

1. Summerfield, "A Critique," 1451.

minimize or disregard these resources, especially when availability of Western health care is minimal, can have tragic consequences.

The previous two chapters have highlighted the suffering narrative of the Lost Boys, specifically and how they have been exposed to cultural, communal, and personal experiences that Western psychologists, and even the Dinka, consider traumatic. As I have noted, upon arrival in the United States, the Lost Boys were well versed in the clinical description of PTSD and its symptomatic criteria. For example, they specifically spoke of nightmares that replayed scenes from the war or the camp, sleeplessness, and what clinicians would call a hyperstartle reflex. Just as in the refugee camp, these experiences were widespread among the resettled refugees, and few had trouble speaking about them. Resettlement agencies were warned that a large percentage of Lost Boys would arrive with PTSD. Indeed, it became an assumed diagnosis.[2] How, though, did the Lost Boys, or more generally the Dinka, learn about this thing we call trauma? Was it already a familiar concept in their own culture? How did they, before being introduced to PTSD by the West, describe behavior that one might exhibit after a frightening and life-threatening event?

Language can help us understand many important aspects of illness in a given culture. So a good question to consider is, does the Dinka culture have a word for anything similar to what we call trauma or PTSD? In short, no they do not. They do, however, distinguish between four other types of emotional distress. *Reare nohom* indicates a state of confusion that lasts for a short duration and can even be momentary. This might describe someone suddenly startled or one who is in what we would call a state of shock characterized by confusion and disorientation. *Aceimol*, on the other hand, indicates a mental distress of a longer, undefined duration. *Marasanom* is an Arabic word that the Dinka have adopted and use to describe the state of sleepwalking. *Jok dhuanb* translates as "the disease of the old ones," or what we might call dementia.[3]

That the Dinka have no language of their own for the phenomena of trauma, in spite of having lived through decades of war, is revealing. It doesn't necessarily mean that the diagnosis of PTSD should never be

2. It is important to note that in spite of this popular application of PTSD as an appropriate diagnosis in the Lost Boy population few were ever seen by mental health professionals, even after arrival in Tennessee.

3. This information was gleaned from discussions with Dinka elders.

applied in their context. But it does, or at least should, reveal a level of tension between indigenous understandings of stress-related behaviors, or what is considered outside the ordinary among the Dinka, and the hardy Western biomedical approach to the same. Some Western views might hold that the Dinka simply have not had the educational means with which to learn about trauma. They don't know that what may seem ordinary during war (nightmares, reliving experiences, and the like) is actually quite problematic. This takes us back to the physician we met in chapter 1 who believes that the Dinka just don't know enough to know what's wrong with themselves.

This extreme describes the one end of a spectrum that holds PTSD as a diagnosis universally applicable to all cultures without making any type of adjustment for culturally specific beliefs or behaviors. On the other end of the spectrum, some argue that the diagnosis of PTSD is itself culturally constructed. Every culture is unique, and care for refugees should be based on attention to cultural difference, environmental influence, and social meaning—not Western psychological models. We will hear more about this perspective in a moment. Still others, such as myself, fall somewhere between the two and believe that other cultures have their own methods of effectively easing psychological distress that should be honored and from which we can learn even in light of PTSD. These three general positions are similar to Emmanuel Lartey's frame presented in chapter 1 for understanding how pastoral care applies strategies across cultures. You may recall that he names the blind importation of Western methodologies as globalization; the honoring of each culture's practice without the influence of Western method as indigenization; and the exchange of methods and ideas, the middle ground, as internationalization.[4]

Posttraumatic Stress Disorder

The Diagnostic and Statistical Manual of Mental Disorders, fourth edition (DSM-IV), defines PTSD by its essential feature: "The development of characteristic symptoms following exposure to an extreme traumatic

4. Lartey, "Globalization," 88–91.

stressor,"[5] and describes a characteristic set of symptoms that include the following:[6]

A. Experiencing a traumatic event in which the life of self or other is threatened with death or injury *and* the individual feels fear, helplessness or horror

B. The traumatic event is reexperienced in *one or more* of these ways: intrusive recollection of the event, dreams of the event; a sense of reliving the experience; psychological distress at cues that symbolize some aspect of the traumatic event; physiological response to the cues representing aspects of a traumatic event

C. Avoidance of stimuli associated with a traumatic event or a numbing of responsiveness as indicated by *three or more* of the following: avoidance of thoughts, feelings or conversation associated with the event; avoidance of activities, places, people that are associated with the traumatic event; inability to recall important aspects of the trauma; diminished interest in significant activities; restricted range of affect; sense of foreshortened future

D. Symptoms of increased arousal indicated by *two* of the following: difficulty sleeping; outbursts of anger; difficulty concentrating; hypervigilance; exaggerated startle response

E. Duration of the disturbance for more than one month

F. The disturbance causes clinically significant distress or impairment in social, occupational, or other functioning

The DSM-IV further notes the following cultural specifications, "Individuals who have recently emigrated from areas of considerable social unrest and civil conflict may have elevated rates of Posttraumatic Stress Disorder. Such individuals may be especially reluctant to divulge experiences of torture and trauma due to their vulnerable political

---

5. First, *Diagnostic and Statistical Manual-IV* (DSM-IV), 424. The DSM is currently under revision with a new version expected in the near future. This revision process is notable for its good-faith effort to include input from cross-cultural research. "One newly proposed negative cognition about the future (for example 'foreshortened future') that comes from cross-cultural research on trauma-related beliefs among Latinos and Southeast Asians is "my soul is gone forever" and "my nervous system is completely ruined" (Friedman, "PTSD," 8).

6. Ibid., 427–29.

immigrant status. Specific assessments of traumatic experiences and con-
comitant symptoms are needed for such individuals."[7]

Judith Herman, a professor of psychiatry with a specialty in the
treatment of trauma, and others also argue for a distinction between
simple PTSD (as symptomatically described above) and a complex
PTSD syndrome.[8] Complex PTSD is especially common among survivors of repeated childhood abuse but also among political detainees,
prisoners of war, and refugees subjected to similar traumatic experiences. Long-term captivity and a sense of physical entrapment accompanied by the perpetrator's coercive control over the victim's daily life
figure prominently among the causes of complex PTSD.[9] Survivors'
suffering may be especially pervasive when the trauma occurs over a
period of time that spans multiple developmental stages of childhood.
Herman notes that this type of severe and repeated trauma may result in
a more fragmented sense of self or, as she says, "a malignant sense of the
self as contaminated, guilty and evil."[10] Also Herman notes that complex PTSD tends to create particular disturbances in the three areas of
symptoms, character, and manner of repeated harm. Christine Courtois
offers a nice summary of the symptoms characteristic of complex PTSD
as proposed by Herman. The list is lengthy but includes alterations in
the ability to regulate affective impulses; alteration in one's perception
of self, the perpetrator, and/or relationship with others; and alteration
in one's systems for making meaning.[11] At the time of Herman's article
(1992), complex PTSD or Disorders of Extreme Stress Not Otherwise
Specified (DESNOS) was under consideration for inclusion in the
DSM-IV. Though many practitioners agree that the PTSD criteria as
they stood in the DSM-III were insufficient, a larger set of criteria for
complex PTSD syndrome was not included in the DSM-IV.[12] Features

7. Ibid., 426.

8. Herman, "Complex PTSD," 87–100. Courtois and others list complex PTSD
and disorders of extreme stress not otherwise specified (DESNOS) as synonymous
(Courtois, "Complex Trauma," 412–25).

9. Herman, "Complex PTSD," 87.

10. Ibid., 95.

11. Symptoms of complex PTSD are currently covered in comorbid conditions
such as Dissociative Disorder (DD), Borderline Personality Disorder (BPD) (Courtois,
"Complex Trauma," 421–25).

12. Ibid.

of complex PTSD are once again under consideration for inclusion in the updated DSM-V due for release in 2012.[13]

Assessment

Diagnosing someone with PTSD requires some type of assessment, which, in the Western context, generally occurs during an intake interview and subsequent counseling sessions with a trained (i.e., university-trained and state-licensed) psychiatrist, psychologist, social worker, or pastoral counselor. In the refugee camp, written assessment tools may also be used even if psychological counseling is not available in any regular form. Some common structured interview tools include the Diagnostic Interview Schedule (DIS), the Structured Clinical Interview for DSM-III (SCID), and the Structured Interview for PTSD (SI-PTSD).[14] A few questionnaires or surveys have been developed or adapted for use with refugee populations that allow for either individual or large-scale assessment of PTSD. These assessment tools also typically require that the assessment be administered and evaluated by a trained professional in order to retain validity of the results. Most prominent among these is the Harvard Trauma Questionnaire, developed by the Harvard Program in Refugee Trauma. This screening tool is available in six versions, including Bosnian, Croatian, Japanese, Laotian, and Vietnamese;[15] each attempts to take into consideration the language and idioms of distress particular to that region.[16] Also frequently used in refugee populations is the Hopkins Symptom Checklist (HSCL-25), designed to measure anxiety and depression. The Harvard Program in Refugee Trauma has translated the HSCL for use in six refugee populations.[17]

A 2002 article by Michael Hollifield et al. attempts to evaluate the reliability of assessment tools as measures of PTSD in refugee populations. By examining published articles in the field, the authors

13. Friedman, "PTSD," 8.

14. Lating et al., "Psychological Assessment."

15. It is important to note that, as in much of the research on PTSD in refugee populations, neither the Harvard Trauma Questionnaire nor the Child Health Questionnaire mentioned at a later point has been validated for use with Sudanese populations.

16. Harvard Program in Refugee Trauma, "Harvard," lines 1–8.

17. The HSCL and manual was translated by the HPRT into Bosnian, Croatian, Cambodian, Japanese, Laotian, and Vietnamese (Harvard Program in Refugee Trauma, "Hopkins," lines 15–16).

identify 125 different instruments (questionnaires, surveys, and inter-view schedules) used to measure refugee trauma and health status.[18] Out of all these articles, only three meet the criteria set in the study. They include the Harvard Trauma Questionnaire (HTQ), Vietnamese Depression Scale (VDS), and an unnamed scale that assesses mental health factors.[19]

Treatment

Common treatment options begin with various forms of supportive talk therapy with a goal of cognitively reframing the traumatic events. Typically, traumatic memories are highly emotionally charged and defy normal attempts to incorporate them into our everyday frame of mean-ing that we use to make sense of the world. Talk therapy attempts to normalize the event in such a way that it can be recalled with a lesser degree of emotion and eventually incorporated into the meaning sys-tem of the individual.

One method especially useful because of its economic and lo-gistical feasibility for large groups (e.g., refugee camps) is Testimony Therapy. This method, used most recently with Bosnian and Sudanese refugees, allows a refugee to tell the trauma story to the acting coun-selor in the form of testimony.[20] The testimony is recorded in written form and presented back to the refugee. Its name, Testimony Therapy, is a bit confusing. At its heart, it is a form of Exposure Therapy, in which exposure to the harrowing events through storytelling, or testimony as it is called in this case, attempts to desensitize the victim to these events. Stuart Lustig et al. claim that creating a testimony is a particu-larly important form of therapy for cultures that have a deep tradition

18. Hollifield et al., "Measuring Trauma," 611–21

19. This study used the criteria developed by Weathers et al. that include a state-ment of purpose, state a defined construct, how the instrument was designed and why, what method and rational was used in its development, report "at least one measure of validity and reliability." They conclude: "The majority of articles about refugee trauma or health are either descriptive or include quantitative data from instruments that have limited or untested validity and reliability in refugees" (Hollifield et al., "Measuring Trauma," 611–21).

20. Lustig et al., "Testimonial Psychotherapy in Adolescent Refugees," 31–45; Weine et al., "Testimony Psychotherapy in Bosnian Refugees," 1720–26

of storytelling.[21] Also, it can shift the focus of therapy from individual pathology to more socially acceptable forms of sociopolitical testimony (important in cultures where therapy is stigmatized). Narrative Exposure Therapy (NET) is a similar approach but combines the storytelling with Cognitive Behavior Therapy (CBT). In other words, it uses cognitive reframing to help organize the traumatic narrative, which can become disjointed, and locates the most debilitating aspects of the traumatic memory. Frank Neuner et al. conducted a study using NET in the treatment of PTSD among a group of Sudanese refugees in a Ugandan refugee camp.[22]

A pilot study conducted in 2004 used Cognitive Behavioral Therapy with Vietnamese refugees suffering from PTSD complicated by panic disorder. Devon Hinton et al. employed a "culturally modified" form of CBT (in addition to pharmacological therapy) that included techniques such as PTSD education, muscle relaxation, visualization, relaxation techniques, and the like.[23] The results of this study indicate that CBT significantly reduced the incidents of somatic pain and related anxiety attacks associated with PTSD.

Yet another treatment option, Eye Movement Desensitization and Reprocessing (EMDR), has a controversial history regarding its effectiveness for use in Western populations. In the practice of EMDR, the clinician prompts the retelling of the traumatic event in conjunction with bilateral eye movements. Joann Rittenhouse states that EMDR resolves trauma "through accessing an innate form of accelerated information processing."[24] Over the course of treatment, the traumatic memories or images are reincorporated in a more positive frame. Success is gauged by client self-assessment, using a measurement specially designed for EMDR therapy.[25] At least one article makes the claim that EMDR is successful in multicultural therapy, though it should be noted that the case study presented in this article involves an individual of Anglo-Mexican

21. Lustig et al., "Testimonial Psychotherapy for Adolescent Refugees," 31–45.

22. Neuner et al., "A Comparison of Narrative Exposure Therapy," 581.

23. Hinton et al., "CBT," 429–33.

24. Rittenhouse, "Using Eye Movement Desensitization," 399–408.

25. These process measures include "ratings of subjective units of distress [SUD] elicited by the fear-provoking images and validity to cognition [VoC] ratings of the new cognitions to be associated with the images" (Davidson and Parker, "Eye Movement," 305–16.

heritage who was raised in the United States. The author makes the unsubstantiated claim that EMDR "may be singularly appropriate for biracial and culturally diverse clients because of its ability to allow the client to frame and explore his or her experiences without a clinician's interpretation."[26] Contrary to this claim, a meta-analysis of EMDR found the treatment technique to be no more effective than other exposure techniques and, further, that the eye movements so central to the treatment are unnecessary.[27]

While this is certainly not an exhaustive list of therapeutic approaches to the treatment of PTSD, it is a selective sampling of some approaches that have been adapted in the treatment of refugees. Just as the analysis of assessment tools should be carefully evaluated, the claims of effectiveness for these approaches in refugee populations should be cautiously reviewed. It is also important to remember that mental health care of refugees can take place in many settings, including refugee camps and locations of repatriation, as well as in a Western context after resettlement occurs. Factors of treatment will vary depending upon the demands of the context.

The Other End of the Spectrum

At the other end of the trauma spectrum are numerous scholars and practitioners who believe that the biomedical paradigms cannot and should not be so easily applied across cultures. Along these lines, I will examine several concepts that critique cross-cultural PTSD assessment and treatment approaches. I will begin with the idea that the PTSD diagnosis creates victims instead of honoring resilience. I will then discuss the idea of category fallacy to address how medical symptoms from one culture can be inappropriately imposed upon another. Next, I will consider the role of justice (or the abandonment thereof) in the treatment of PTSD. Though often overlooked in favor of focusing on past trauma, the importance of environment and current life circumstances as an essential element of refugee psychological care will be my next point of concern.

Some professionals in the field of transcultural psychology are quite critical of the use of Western psychological paradigms in other

26. Rittenhouse, "Using Eye Movement Desensitization," 399–408.

27. Davidson and Parker, "Eye Movement," 305–16.

cultures. Even the definition of PTSD reveals certain embedded assumptions. For example, "characteristic" symptoms implies a normative set of criteria while "symptoms" serves to define the field of inquiry as a medical one substantiated by (Western) scientific reasoning. Likewise, "extreme traumatic stressor" implies both a quantitative and qualitative measure. For these critics, PTSD as a diagnosis is culturally and historically bound.[28] Thus, when applied to other cultures, such a diagnosis is, to them, nothing less than the "medicalization" and "universalization" of behaviors or experiences with otherwise culturally specific meaning.[29] In other words, diagnosis becomes a process of reshaping culturally specific behaviors so they fit into a medical frame of understanding. Once this is accomplished, the results can be considered, as is physical disease, to be universally defined.

Derek Summerfield, a prominent critic of intercultural PTSD, proposes that PTSD served to create a social shift in the popular consciousness after the Vietnam War; this shift cemented it as the diagnosis of choice for years to come. He suggests that the diagnosis of PTSD among Vietnam veterans shifted the social roles of veterans from that of perpetrators (of war atrocities) to victims. Summerfield writes, "Post-traumatic stress disorder legitimized their 'victimhood,' gave them moral exculpation, and guaranteed them a disability pension because the diagnosis could be attested to by a doctor; this was a potent combination."[30] Not surprising is that Summerfield also uses this idea of creating victimhood in his critique of applying the diagnosis of PTSD to refugee populations.

Summerfield is among the most vocal opponents of the universal application of PTSD. He offers a critique of several assumptions foundational to psychosocial programs that address PTSD in refugee populations. Among these assumptions is the idea that war is an extreme circumstance that results in something called traumatization, which in turn carries with it expansive and imprecise definitions that imply a pathological condition applicable to large populations. Second is the belief that "there is a universal human response to highly stressful

28. Young, *The Harmony*, 5.
29. Summerfield, "The Invention," 95–98.
30. Ibid.

events, captured by Western psychological frameworks."[31] While war certainly creates psychological stressors on its victims, he says, nonvalidated tools designed to assess levels of PTSD in survivors of war tend to overestimate the numbers of those needing treatment and grossly neglect the elements of resilience that allow war survivors to continue with a meaningful life. In a statement that reminds us once again of the tension between the prominent focus on the individual in the biomedical paradigms and the power and value of the social or collective meaning, Summerfjeld writes:

> Human responses to war are not analogous to physical trauma: people do not passively register the impact of external forces . . . but engage with them in an active and problem-solving way. Suffering arises from, and is resolved in a social context, shaped by the meanings and understandings applied to events. The distinctiveness of the experience of war or torture lies in these meanings and not in a biopsychomedical paradigm. This is not just a conceptual issue, but also an ethical one, given the danger of misunderstanding and indeed dehumanizing survivors via reductionist labeling. Helping agencies have a duty to recognize distress, but also to attend to what the people carrying the distress want to signal by it. War affected populations are largely directing their attention not inwards, to their mental processes, but outwards, to their devastated social world. They know that they will stand or fall by what they do in and about that world.[32]

Mike Wessells, a psychologist who researches war trauma in children of various cultures, isolates at least two distinct problems with applying PTSD in Western biomedical terms.[33] First, he agrees that PTSD diagnosis focuses upon the impact on an individual victim, with

---

31. The other assumptions that Summerfield addresses include the following: "*Large numbers of victims traumatized by war need professional help*"; "*Western psychological approaches are relevant to violent conflict worldwide*"; "*Victims do better if they emotionally ventilate and 'work through' their experience*"; "*There are vulnerable groups and individuals who need to be specifically targeted for psychological help*"; "*Wars represent a mental health emergency; rapid intervention can prevent the development of serious mental problems, as well as subsequent violence and wars*"; "*Local workers are overwhelmed and may themselves be traumatised*" (Summerfield, "A Critique," 1455–57, italics original).

32. Ibid., 1449–62 (italics original).

33. Wessels, "Culture, Power, and Community," 269–70.

little or no attention given to the communal aspects associated with the trauma of war. In many non-Western cultures, separating the individual from the community in such a manner distorts the concept of the self and ignores the collective aspects of trauma that shape, sometimes quite deeply, a culture's social existence. Second, Wessells proposes that Western DSM criteria single out a specific PTSD event (or multiple events) without appreciation for or consideration of the broader historical context. This can, consequently, deny the associated forces of oppression that make up a significant part of one's social reality.[34] These points will be especially important when we attempt to interpret trauma in the Dinka population. The focus on who they are as individuals comes only in the midst of the collective forces of nation, tribe, clan, and family. For the Lost Boys, the story of the trauma they endured must be understood in the context of a long history of political and religious oppression of the Dinka people. Only in this way can one truly comprehend the importance of particular traumatic events as they unfolded. If a treatment approach for PTSD fails to consider these social, historical, and political contexts of trauma, it opens the door for a distorted understanding of symptoms, treatment options, and research-outcome data.

Assessment of Trauma in Other Cultures

One way to understand the application of PTSD in the Dinka culture, even though they don't have a language for it, is what psychiatrist and medical anthropologist Arthur Kleinman calls "category fallacy." He describes this as the misapplication of disease symptoms from the culture in which the diagnosis was developed to another. He writes, "Category fallacy is the reification of a nosological category developed for a particular cultural group that is then applied to members of another culture for whom it lacks coherence and its validity has not been established."[35] A more concrete example of this might help us. While the Lost Boys may complain about reoccurring dreams of a traumatic event, many African tribes explain this in more culturally relational terms. For example, as one tribal elder proposed in an interview, the dreams keep coming back because that individual has failed to make

34. Ibid., 269.
35. Kleinman, "Anthropology and Psychiatry," 452.

reparations for a wrong committed against another. Or another elder suggested that the body pain experienced by so many of the Lost Boys comes from the mournful longing of a mother who grieves because of their separation. While most of us in the West would think of the Lost Boys' physical pain (after having been medically cleared) as a psychosomatic symptom of the emotional loss of his mother, in doing so we miss the depth of the relational meaning within the Dinka explanation. In other words, the pain exists because the mother and child are relationally connected in such a way that the pain felt by the mother at the loss of her son is expressed in dual locations: in the mother's body and the son's body.[36] Category fallacy, Kleinman claims, "occurs routinely in cross-cultural psychiatric research . . . by the imposition of Western categories in societies for which they lack coherence and validity."[37]

Justice and PTSD

Generally speaking, biomedical approaches to the treatment of PTSD in refugee populations also do not address the issue of justice or redress for the harm caused by the perpetrators of violence. However, in light of the aims of the Truth and Reconciliation Commission in South Africa and the Bosnia War Crimes Tribunal, it seems relevant to ask, what role does justice play in the process of recovery from PTSD? Some would say that the issue of justice has no bearing on modern therapeutic techniques in the treatment of PTSD. One of Derek Summerfield's strongest critiques of Western biomedical diagnosis of PTSD is that instead of highlighting the resilience and adaptability of refugees, PTSD creates an environment in which the refugee must claim his or her victimhood and acquiesce to (or accept and incorporate) the injustices inflicted in order to move toward healing.[38] Resistance to this, in biomedical vernacular, is understood as pathological. Therapy of this sort he describes as an ethos of acceptance and goes on to say:

> Victims of war may have to struggle with whether "recovery" and "acceptance" are merely markers of their own impotence and humiliation or whether, worse still, they are an acquiescence

36. This is one of the ways that the elders in Kakuma Refugee Camp explained bodily pain with no apparent organic origin.

37. "Anthropology and Psychiatry," 452.

38. Summerfield, "The Invention," 381–88.

in injustice by themselves, by people they know, and, frequently, by the Western led world order that, behind the rhetorical
screen of "human rights," retains the realpolitik of "business
as usual." Trauma programmes certainly can be seen cynically
by those for whom they are intended, they can be experienced
as patronizing or indeed as a form of pacification. In Bosnia,
people derisively referred to the aid delivered to them through
a model that did not offer physical protection, restitution, or
justice as "bread and counseling."[39]

We will see shortly, in testimony to these very critiques, that the resilience of the Dinka is rooted in community, a sense of justice, and a faith
that, in defiance of victimhood, helps them sustain a sense of agency.

Middle Ground

Richard Mollica and others take an approach to treatment of refugees
that stands between the extremes of the universal application of PTSD
diagnosis (without regard to cultural context) and an anthropological
stance that eschews the transcultural use of Western paradigms. They
propose that science-based refugee studies are needed to determine appropriate factors of mental health treatment, including PTSD, in refugee populations. Of utmost importance in this effort is to investigate
the environment in which refugees live (i.e., the refugee camp) as well
as the individual trauma. Mollica, a psychiatrist firmly entrenched in
the biomedical culture, calls for the narrowing of criteria for determining psychological diagnosis to prevent the overgeneralized application
of pathological distress to all refugees because of their circumstances.
Mollica and his colleagues write, "There has been a tendency to expand
the definition of mental health outcomes away from narrowly defined
psychiatric disorders to broader categories that describe the psychological distress of refugees in nonclinical terms."[40] In fact, this study does
much to reveal the resilience of refugees. Mollica et al. propose policy
recommendations for refugee camps that can serve as preventative
measures to overall depression and PTSD. In particular, they suggest
"[the creation of] programs that support work, indigenous religious

---

39. Summerfield, "Effects of War," 381–88. See the section called "War as Illness or
Social Problem."

40. Mollica et al., "Science-Based Policy," 158–66.

practices, and culture-based altruistic behavior among refugees."[41] Specifically, Cambodian refugees in this study who participated in religious activities (public or private) were "one-third as likely to have PTSD" as those who did not; refugees who had some opportunity to work were less likely to be depressed; and there is a positive psychological effect when refugees have the ability and opportunity to care for others, though the responsibility of caring for others (e.g., the elderly) may have stressful effects as well.[42] Mollica et al. close their article with a rather startling summary recommendation that highlights refugee resilience rather than the frequent biomedical approach that focuses on the treatment of a pathological condition. They write, "[This] analysis does suggest the therapeutic potential of shifting away from the field's previous emphasis on trauma to those psychosocial factors that can be appropriately encouraged or minimized in the refugee setting based on appreciation of their beneficial or harmful mental health effects."[43]

The Impact of Environment on Symptoms and Treatment

As we have seen with the Lost Boys, the life of a refugee moves through several stages of vulnerability, each of which can have a psychological effect, PTSD notwithstanding. These factors may present themselves in ways the can affect treatment of PTSD. I have described two phases of refugee life for the Lost Boys, including flight and the refugee camp. In this chapter, we also focus somewhat on a third phase: resettlement. The refugee camp and resettlement pose different obstacles and create different psychological stressors on refugees.

The first problem one encounters in the refugee-camp setting is the extreme lack of safety with which the refugees must continue to live. Judith Herman suggests that the first stage of healing for all who are recovering from trauma requires establishing a safe place and relative control over one's body and life.[44] In reality, such control and safety do not exist in the refugee camp.

Second, the assessment tools and treatments listed earlier in the chapter become nonsensical in the context of Kakuma Refugee Camp,

41. Ibid.
42. Ibid.
43. Ibid.
44. Herman, *Trauma and Recovery*, 159–64.

which has only one psychiatrist and one psychologist to care for eighty thousand refugees. Even if we consider the few hundred refugees who have been minimally trained to provide psychoeducation among the greater refugee population, this hardly meets criteria for Western-designed assessment and treatment protocols.

The life circumstances of a refugee going through the arduous re-settlement process are as important as the environment in the refugee camp in terms of preventing or treating psychological distress. To approach the treatment of PTSD in refugees going through the resettlement process with a primary focus on incorporating past traumatic events risks overlooking the ongoing stressors that can create additional psychological symptoms or exacerbate ongoing PTSD symptoms. Carlos Gonsalves, working primarily with Latin American refugees in the process of resettlement, identifies five stages of the resettlement process. I have listed them with corresponding psychological symptoms in the table below.

Table 4.1: Psychological Stages of the Refugee Resettlement Process[45]

RESETTLEMENT STAGE	PSYCHOLOGICAL FACTORS
Early Arrival	Difficulty focusing conversation, little energy, depression, express a sense of loss
Destabilization	Anger, complaints, resistance to socio-cultural change, lack of social intimacy, loneliness
Exploration and Restabilization	Feeling isolated, marital conflict
Return to Normal Life	Delayed grief, painful feelings and memories, depression
Decompensation Stage	Psychotic delusions, suicide, heightened alcohol use

Gonsalves proposes that the psychological factors of each of these stages may coexist with issues of PTSD but carry significant psychic weight in and of themselves and so require context-specific strategies of intervention.

---

45. This table is my own creation using information taken from Gonsalves, "Psychological Stages," 382–89.

Another Perspective

Another significant way that Western psychologists talk about PTSD and its effect upon the individual is through trauma theory—what is happening in the inner world of the individual in the midst of trauma? One such theory considers trauma as a disorganization of one's assumptive world.[46] In particular, Ronnie Janoff-Bulman notes three innate perceptions of self in the world that constitute what she calls core assumptions. [47] The first assumption is that the world is a good place. She includes both people and events that are seen as benevolent in intent in this concept of world. Second, the world is meaningful; and third, the self is worthy.[48]

To explain the development of one's assumptive world, Janoff-Bulman proposes that the child who grows in a caring and trusting environment learns that he or she can trust others and the world. Janoff-Bulman's idea is not only a claim that one can trust others and the world, but also a value judgment that the world is good, and, therefore, that one is deserving of good things from the world in return. Janoff-Bulman suggests that one lives in the world with not only core assumptions but also assumptive expectations.

Unfortunately, Janoff-Bulman does not give sufficient attention to the core assumptions of the self in relation to others. Yes, she acknowledges that a benevolent world includes the people with whom one interacts. She lacks, though, a core value that reflects the self's responsibility, even positive obligation, to the community and vice versa. Without it, such core assumptions are incomplete for cultures like that of the Dinka, who heavily on their connection to the community for survival and fulfillment.

At first glance, these assumptions seem framed within the context of the industrialized world, where many have a relative sense (or illusion) of control and are relatively free from basic types of danger that threaten life in less-developed countries, such as famine, wild animals, war, and the like. The value judgment that one is deserving of good re-

---

46. Everly and Lating, *Psychotraumatology: Key Papers*, 76.

47. Janoff-Bulman's concept of core assumptions builds on the work of several preceding theories of personal belief systems including those of J. Bowlby, G. Kelly, and S. Epstein, among others. See Janoff-Bulman, *Shattered Assumptions*, 177.

48. Ibid., 6.

wards from the external world seems, likewise, to stem from arrogance, of sorts, particularly characteristic of Western culture. I am ever aware that refugees around the world may not claim that the world is good or that it owes them some favorable reward. Nor do I assume, even with the most privileged of upbringings, that they feel the world to be ordinarily a safe place. Yet, while they might not articulate it as such, there does seem to be an underlying belief that what has happened to them is unjust. If the world does not offer them the good they deserve, certainly they expect that help will come from somewhere. Even in the refugee camp, facing starvation, disease, and continued violence, though they have few resources to compare their own plight with that of others around the world, they express the belief that, at the very least, they should not be suffering.

Janoff-Bulman names the core assumption of a benevolent world (including people and events) and proposes that people believe a meaningful world is one that is just and controllable. Traumatic experience threatens to inflict violence and harm in ways that defy any attempt to create meaning. Elaine Scarry proposes that "war is the massive fact of itself a huge structure for the derealization of cultural constructs"— thus, it is the function of war to put reality, as she phrases it, "up for grabs."[49] Herman, sums up the effects of trauma this way: "Traumatic events call into question basic human relationships. They breach the attachments of family, friendship, love and community. They shatter the construction of the self that is formed and sustained in relation to others. They undermine the belief systems that give meaning to human experience. They violate the victim's faith in a natural or divine order and cast the victim into a state of existential crisis."[50] Interesting, as we will see later, it that just such a breach of community, because of a deep moral obligation of care that grounds very specific cultural and spiritual practices, the Dinka manage to avoid.

Summary

In this chapter I have tried to highlight both the current Western understanding of PTSD and some of the tensions or difficulties with applying PTSD diagnosis and treatment to refugee populations. This is

49. Scarry, *The Body in Pain*, 137.

50. Herman, *Trauma and Recovery*, 51.

by no means exhaustive in either respect but will be helpful to us as we prepare to discuss the resilience of the Lost Boys.

The DSM-IV has a clear set of criteria for determining the diagnosis of PTSD. It is less clear that assessment tools have been developed to make adequate adjustments for culture and language. At least a few assessment questionnaires, however, have been tested for validity in certain populations. Clearly the Harvard Program in Refugee Trauma currently leads the field in this respect. Similar problems arise in relation to treatment strategies for refugees. Some studies show that psychodynamic talk therapy, Testimony Therapy, Cognitive Behavioral Therapy, Narrative Exposure Therapy, and Eye Movement Desensitization and Reprocessing Therapy have proven successful within refugee populations. One is left, though, with the realization that the field of refugee studies is still so new that the methods of treatment have yet to withstand the test of time. Treatment conducted in the refugee camp is hampered by continued threats to the safety of refugees and by the inability of researchers to follow up with long-term results.

Critics of Western psychologists' method of applying a PTSD diagnosis to refugee populations draw from a long list of anthropological resources. Prominent points of critique include that PTSD should be understood as a diagnosis for a particular time and place and is not universally applicable across cultures. Also, PTSD focuses on the assessment and treatment of ways in which refugees are victims instead of on their resilience. The anthropological approach to understanding trauma shows how PTSD diagnosis may require that one claim victimhood and surrender justifiable feelings of anger, resentment, and demands for justice. Agencies may rush to offer psychosocial services to victims of war, but the list of countries that demand justice is very short indeed. In other words, treatment for refugees comes, according to critics, at the cost of justice.

The Harvard Program in Refugee Trauma suggests that instead of keeping such a narrow focus on the traumatic events of the past, helping agencies may better serve refugees by tending to issues in the everyday environment of the refugee camp that mitigate psychological stressors. Likewise it is important to be mindful of the stage of resettlement and consequent psychological stressors associated with the postmigration period. Finally, critics of cross-cultural PTSD diagnosis note the absence of physical symptoms in the diagnostic criteria even though practitioners generally agree that those suffering from PTSD often present with accompanying somatic complaints. Standard definitions imply that somatic symptoms are repressed emotions that need to be verbalized. This overlooks, however, the dynamics of language, power, and pain in many cultures, including this one. Elaine Scarry proposes that pain can never be fully expressed, and that narrative in Western medical culture is primarily dismissed. Many cultures understand somatic pain not necessarily as a psychological aberration of the individual but often as the result of a relational (social) rupture that cannot by rectified by the individual alone.

I stated in the beginning that it is not my intention to prove or disprove PTSD but rather to illumine the knotty problems that arise whenever one crosses cultures unprepared for the differences one will encounter. So if we leave this chapter with more questions than answers about applying Western methods of diagnosis and assessment of PTSD to other cultures, I think it is a good thing. Now we turn again to examine the Lost Boys and their remarkable resilience in spite of multiple indicators that they have suffered from PTSD.

5

Building Community Resilience

On the day we arrived an eagle was spotted in the area that eventually came to land in the government compound under the flag of South Sudan. The eagle, they say, vomited blood. This caused great concern because it was seen as a sign that "blood will be shed." The elders were summoned so that they could pray for peace and to keep the fighting away from Bor.

—Field notes from Bor, Sudan

BASED ON THE STORY OF THE LOST BOYS' JOURNEY OF EScape and life in a refugee camp, it is not surprising that aid workers were concerned about the effects of trauma and even PTSD. Indeed, the sixty Lost Boys resettled in Nashville arrived with heart-wrenching stories of the many traumatic events they endured. A survey of 273 Lost Boy minors resettled in the United States reveals the following war-related experiences:[1]

Table 5.1: Lost Boys' Traumatic Experiences

Witnessed torture of family or friends	60 percent
Witnessed injury of family or friends	74 percent
Witnessed killing of family or friends	76 percent

1. This table is my own creation using information from Geltman et al., "The 'Lost Boys of Sudan,'" 587.

Experienced torture themselves	20 percent
Injury to self	29 percent
Near drowning	47 percent
Near suffocation	32 percent
Head trauma	31 percent
Loss of consciousness	26 percent

This list does not include even more common experiences, such as food deprivation and daily threat of harm endured in the refugee camp. In the same study, 241 Lost Boys who completed the Harvard Trauma Questionnaire indicated that the following symptoms of PTSD were prevalent:[2]

Table 5.2: Lost Boys' Trauma Symptoms

"Feeling as though event were happening again"	40 percent
Having recurrent nightmares	38 percent
Feeling on guard	37 percent
Responding suddenly and emotionally when reminded of the hurtful event	37 percent
Avoiding activities that remind them of the hurtful event	36 percent
Avoiding thoughts associated with the hurtful event	32 percent

To make matters even more complicated for refugees, premigration responses to trauma can be exacerbated by postresettlement depression. This, in turn, can substantially complicate the multitude of hurdles faced by refugees in the first years of resettlement, creating a cycle of distress and dependence. If we think of this in terms of PTSD, Ellen Heptinstall and others note that "post-migration factors said to put PTSD sufferers at greater risk of continued and increased psychological distress included delays in processing refugee applications, obstacles to employment, language problems, racial discrimination and loneliness."[3] Given all of this information, it is not surprising that resettlement workers in Nashville were prepared in advance for a high level of dysfunction that mental health workers warned could result

2. This table is my own creation using information derived from Geltman et al., "The 'Lost Boys of Sudan,'" 587.

3. Heptinstall et al., "PTSD and Depression in Refugee Children," 377–80.

from trauma, especially when experienced at such a young age as was the case for the Lost Boys.

In spite of this, what was most significant was not the level of dysfunction but rather the high degree of *resilience* demonstrated by the Lost Boys who arrived. In other words, to whatever level traumatic experiences may have created long-term emotional distress in the Lost Boys, in most it did not appear to result in a significant degree of impairment to "normal" functioning. The majority were able to maintain long-term employment, attend school, and adjust to a new culture within a very short period of time. As early as 1994, Swedish Save the Children, which ran a mental health program for the unaccompanied minors in one of the refugee camps, reported "very low numbers of children with serious psychiatric symptoms who needed institutional care"; and UNICEF also noted a remarkable resilience among the same population.[4] Evidence of this resilience bears itself out over the larger population of Lost Boys resettled across the United States as well. The following table, provided by the Office of Refugee Resettlement (ORR) in a report to Congress, indicates the employment level for the Lost Boys sixteen years and older in the year 2002 (two years after the resettlement process began):

Table 5.3: Employment Status of the Lost Boys [and Girls] by Sex: 2002 Survey[5]

	Employment Rate (EPR) in Percents			Labor Force Participation Rate in Percents			Unemployment Rate in Percents		
Gender	All	Male	Female	All	Male	Female	All	Male	Female
Lost Boys	73.5	74.5	50	88.2	89.4	66.7	14.7	14.9	16.7
U.S. Rates	66.6	69.7	56.3	67.8	74.8	61.3	5.8	5.9	5.6

4. Goodman, "Coping with Trauma," 1177–96; Zutt, *Children of War*.

5. This table was originally headed "Employment Status of the Lost Boys by Sex: 2002 Survey." "Reasons for unemployment among Lost Boys sixteen and older included limited English (88.9 percent), attending school (77.8 percent), and poor health (22.2 percent) (This table is reprinted from the United States Department of Health and Human Services, "Office of Refugee," where it is called Table III-1.) It can be found online: http://www.acf.hhs.gov/programs/orr/data/02arc9.htm#6.

The report reveals that the employment rate among Lost Boys (in the United States for up to two years) is nearly 10 percent higher than the U.S. average and 15 percent higher than the employment rate for the five-year refugee population (refugees who had been in the United States for five years). Furthermore, 60.8 percent of the young men attended English as a Second Language (ESL) classes in addition to regular school;[6] Lost Boys earned higher hourly wages closer to those of the five-year refugee population; and 55.9 percent of the Lost Boys were "attending some type of school or university with nearly 6 percent obtaining a degree since arrival as early as 1999."[7]

These statistics paint a very different picture from the one frequently portrayed, in which the Lost Boys are overwhelmed by PTSD symptoms and unable to negotiate the challenges of building a new life. Psychologist Janice Goodman conducted a study of Lost Boys' coping strategies and noted the sense of empowerment with which they faced their future. She says, "each looked forward to a future that he could shape. The tone of the [trauma] narratives was not bitter. Instead, feelings of brotherliness, kindness, and hope prevailed."[8]

How are we to reconcile this resilient strength with the evidence of potentially debilitating PTSD symptoms suggested in chapter 4? I propose that the community of Lost Boys functions in certain ways to mitigate the symptoms of PTSD. Let me be clear: I do not claim that the Lost Boys do not have experiences that are commonly considered to be symptoms of PTSD. I think, indeed, they do experience many reactions that fit into these categories. But they also have a community of brothers, and some sisters, who behave in a particular manner that serves to foster resilience against the damage that so often makes these reactions debilitating.[9] First and foremost, they act in a way that reflects a profound sense of obligation, a moral obligation of care grounded in their familial and cultural connection to each other and God. This sense

6. It is likely that this percentage includes some Lost Boys who are attending ESL classes while also working full time.

7. "Employment Status of the Lost Boys," lines 56–59.

8. Goodman, "Coping with Trauma," 1177–96.

9. The Lost Boys often refer to themselves as brothers though they are not related by blood. The term *brother* carries with it, though, all of the obligations of one family member toward another.

of obligation is the seedbed from which other practices of healing and resilience emerge.

The Lost Boys learned to (1) create a safe space among each other, (2) articulate justice, and (3) create a collective trauma story. These communal functions emerge from traditions deeply rooted in the Dinka culture as well as from cultural adaptations made under conditions of war. Though I list each function separately, great overlap exists between them, as we will see throughout this chapter and into the next.

These long-held practices and traditions have been folded into their Christian belief. In this context, it is their faith narrative, a narrative framed by the larger Christian story, which, in the end, serves as the greatest of all sources of resilience. Though I will discuss this faith narrative in the next chapter, I introduce it here because it serves as the horizon against which these three practices can best be understood. For the Dinka, rituals and traditions that influence, even unconsciously, their care and obligation toward one another are always held in the context of God, who works through history to bring hope to those in need. This is how they make sense of their world and bring meaning to their own suffering.

Communal Obligation

The idea of communal obligation may raise questions for those of us more accustomed to an individualistic Western culture. What does this obligation look like? How do we know it when we see it? What is at the root of this obligation? Is it simply a deep sense of empathy and compassion working together, or is it something more coercive at work? Among the Dinka, communal obligation is hardly coercive; rather, it's a natural response to the communal other. Far from diminishing a sense of self, such connection to the community strengthens it. Pastoral theologian Emmanuel Lartey notes an essential African perspective when he says, "a communal view of life prevails that emphasizes a sense of belonging, rather than an individualistic one that values aloneness."[10]

The following story of how a small group of Lost Boys negotiated the logistics of car ownership after arrival in the United States offers a glimpse of how this sense of obligation works. A church volunteer was working with a group of Lost Boy refugees who had arrived less than a

10. Lartey, "Globalization," 101.

year earlier. The church community was acting as a surrogate family for four young men by helping them with the practical elements of starting a life in a new country (furniture, clothes, food, and transportation). The church had just purchased a car that would provide these Lost Boys with transportation to and from work. The volunteer gathered the young men together and explained something called a car title, and that one of them would need to sign this title to be the legal owner of the vehicle. He assured them that the car could be shared equally by all (who had licenses) even if only one person signed the title. After only a moment of looking at each other, all four refused to sign. The volunteer was adamant: someone needed to sign the title so that they could use the car to get to work. In fact, having a car would increase the opportunity for better employment because they would no longer be confined to jobs on the bus line. Still, they refused.

Imagine their dilemma. On the one hand, someone, an (American) elder, whom they trust very much, has said that one of them must take ownership of the car. On the other hand, they are obligated to the Dinka community (in this case, to the other three young men). This obligation makes it unthinkable that one should own something that the others do not. To accept this car would deeply wound the communal sense of mutuality among them.

Fortunately, the volunteer was wise enough to ask why there was a problem and approached the question with respect for the Dinka way of understanding the world. With a shift in perspective, he then suggested that one of them think about sacrificing for the sake of the others by taking ownership of the car. He asked, would one be willing to bear the shame of betraying the community so that all could benefit from use of the car? After a moment, the eldest among them stepped forward to sign the title.

In spite of this wonderful story, it would be a mistake to believe that among the Lost Boys no sense of individual ownership exists or that no individual ever has desires for material possessions over and above the group. But this obligation not to exceed the needs of the group remains an underlying philosophy that governs their interactions and care for the other. Concerning issues as important as a car, the sense of communal obligation takes on a very literal form. The community negotiates the less essential, day-to-day experiences of desire and care with the communal obligation that states: another will never be in need of something that I can share.

It should be noted that other African traditions also share this sense of communal obligation and may help us better grasp its broader understanding. For example, it is found in the concept of *ubuntu* that figures so prominently in the theology of bishop Desmond Tutu. Tutu describes *ubuntu* in this way:

> In Africa recognition of our interdependence is called ubuntu in Nguni languages . . . It is the essence of being human. It speaks of the fact that my humanity is caught up and inextricably bound up in yours. I am human because I belong . . . A person with ubuntu is welcoming, hospitable, warm and generous, willing to share . . . They know that they are diminished when others are humiliated, diminished when others are oppressed . . . The quality of ubuntu gives people resilience, enabling them to survive and emerge still human despite all efforts to dehumanize them.[11]

What concerns us particularly in the case of the Lost Boys is how they hold to these obligations in ways that help them negotiate the stresses of displacement and vulnerability.

Moral Obligation of Care

This communal obligation is in fact a moral obligation to care among the Dinka. It is an exercise of justice that shows itself in two forms, equitable concern and retribution. This notion, as we have just seen, that one should have only as much as the other is the driving force behind equitable concern. The Dinka go to great lengths to share what is plentiful among their own clans. Even Dinka refugees resettled in the United States are driven by equitable concern to provide for relatives in refugee camps and southern Sudan by sending money for food, dowries, medicine, and other needs. These remittances can demand a high percentage of their income and make the process of becoming self-sufficient quite a challenge. Nonetheless, the obligation is so overwhelming that many Lost Boys work two or three jobs to pay rent and remittances. Dinka are culturally responsible for assisting numerous degrees of extended family. Unfortunately, over time, as a matter of practicality, many will be

11. Tutu, with Abrams, *God Has a Dream*, 26.

forced to limit access to extended family as a means to reduce requests for what can become unreasonable amounts of money.

During the war, this form of the moral obligation of care may have been one of the most important elements that helped the Lost Boys survive. As they fled across Sudan, even the smallest bits of food were shared. I recall one newly arrived Lost Boy preparing for a job interview shortly after arriving in the United States. He was asked what experiences in his young life could demonstrate dedication and hard work that might make an employer want to hire him. He told of being five years old when he first fled Sudan. His job was to carry the large cooking pot so that when they found food, it could be cooked. Anyone who has ever taken a five-year-old on a long outing can surely appreciate what hard work this was for the youngster. Hundreds of boys and girls ate from that pot. What is had by one is shared by all.

Dinka justice also sometimes takes the less-attractive form of retribution. Violations of equitable concern as well as nonintentional wounding lead to the need for retributive justice. The previous story has an interesting twist on the notion of retribution. In the previous example concerning the car, the cost of retribution for the act of owning more than the others is shame—a cost borne gladly over the alternative of greed. The Dinka will argue especially furiously for retribution when one has been victimized, whether intentionally or through some careless act. Yet, even this has a protocol in the effort to prevent the eruption of violence within and among clans. When I was in Sudan, I witnessed just such an encounter. As we traveled to a distant village, the truck in which we were riding, driven by an overeager and underattentive teenager, struck and killed a goat as it crossed the road. A contingent of elders from our truck along with the driver went to find the owner. From the truck, I could hear the shouting and arguing accompanied by furious looks and threatening gestures, indicating they had, indeed, found him. Because we were traveling to a remote area, several from our party were armed with guns. I was concerned that the event would escalate to a skirmish of open gunfire. Ultimately, it did not. After the matter was settled, begrudgingly to all it seemed, and just restitution paid, I expressed my concern to one of the elders. He assured me that such arguments seldom rise to the level of physical violence between Dinka. While killing an enemy may be not only condoned but seen as heroic, it is considered to be the most egregious offense to kill another Dinka.

Certainly, this is an idyllic vision of life among the Dinka. There are many examples, particularly volatile episodes of violence in the refugee camp, of how this vision has been compromised by war and displacement. Nonetheless, in large but imperfect measure the moral obligation of care provides boundaries of behavior intended to maximize justice and minimize violence within the clan.

Let me say a word here about justice and retribution in times of conflict with "outsiders." When the Dinka stand against an enemy, they do so with a great sense of self-righteousness and often a great deal of violence, especially when tangling with a long-held enemy. In an unstable environment lacking an agency of law enforcement, the Dinka will act according to the rules of their communal sense of justice. In the sometimes-tenuous security of South Sudan, this exacerbates existing tensions and for foreigners may tarnish the image of justice-loving Dinka.

Shortly before my arrival in Bor, Sudan, in the summer of 2008, a small group of Dinka attacked several patients in the hospital run by Médicins Sans Frontières (Doctors Without Borders), killing three adults. According to the Dinka with whom I spoke, the ones killed in this incident were from the Murle tribe, seeking treatment for gunshot wounds received in a raid.[12] The Murle are one of several tribes known throughout the region for their practice of raiding cattle and abducting children, who are then usually sold into slavery. Apparently, one of the Dinka recognized a young woman with the Murle as a cousin who had been kidnapped years before. The Dinka demanded that the hospital authorities turn the young woman over to them. Hospital officials encouraged the Dinka to file a complaint with the police because they did not have the authority to release her to anyone other than those with whom she came. That night a band of Dinka attacked the hospital, taking the young woman and killing the Murle tribe members. This event was tragic not only for the loss of life but also because it precipitated the departure of Médecins Sans Frontiéres from Bor along with much-needed medical care.

While many Dinka I spoke with now publicly disavow actual displays of violence such as the one described, most all continue to espouse what I would describe as a narrative of retribution used to maintain

12. It is common belief that Al-Bashir has and continues to use the Murle to create instability in communities of South Sudan.

the obligation of care. It seems all too easy in these circumstances for fair restitution to decline toward retaliation. In the end, justice in conflict zones is a messy thing challenged by contradictions and unsure boundaries.

Moral Obligation Developed through Multiple Networks of Care

Edward Farley, in his book *Good and Evil: Interpreting a Human Condition*, introduces a similar type of moral responsibility in the concept of compassionate obligation as the center point of his theological anthropology. It is the response to the face of the other that draws forth not merely compassion, a suffering with, but an obligation, a suffering for. He writes, "As the disposition to join with the other in her or his fragile struggles against whatever threatens and violates, obligation is on behalf of."[13] Janice Goodman notes this sense of obligation in her research on coping among the Sudanese youth (Lost Boys). She writes, "The notion of selfhood in which one has responsibility for others, and even exists for the other, provided the impetus for many of the boys to continue their difficult journey, to not give up, and to plan for their future."[14] The care for each other and the obligation to the community as a whole serve to mitigate the overwhelming sense of isolation and helplessness often experienced by victims of trauma. The communal obligation pulls each Lost Boy from the experiences of the past into the reality of the present and onward toward a future filled with hope.

The development of this self-identity bound to the care of the other begins at birth when a child is brought into an intricate system of caretaking among siblings, grandparents, and "stepmothers." Certainly two decades of war have influenced this process of childrearing, but the underlying commitment to familial and communal care remains intact.

A Dinka mother, like a mother in the West, juggles many roles. Not only is she the primary caregiver for the children, but she is responsible for a multitude of household chores as well as the tending of crops grown near the home. For families who own large plots of land planted with corn or sorghum, such work requires the help of the entire family. Men, in general, have little to do with childrearing but tend to the cattle if they are lucky enough to own any in these lean postwar

13. Farley, *Good and Evil*, 42–43.

14. Goodman, "Coping with Trauma," 1183.

days. Because women are seldom left with idle time, children are born into a busy life.[15]

For the first year or so, the infant travels swaddled onto the back of the mother as she moves through the chores and other tasks of the day. When the child becomes hungry, he or she is given the breast wherever they happen to be at the time. For the Dinka, as in many non-Western cultures, breastfeeding is a natural event and requires no undue modesty. It is not unusual for mothers to provide a breast for a hungry child in the midst of a public gathering. In most cases, especially in rural areas, canned formula and baby bottles are not available, so there is no opportunity for the father to help with feeding. Nor is it, traditionally, his place to do so. Much of the care of the young child, especially after the first year, will belong to the extended family, including co-wives, often described as stepmothers, grandmothers, cousins, and siblings. Even very young children may be given charge over a younger brother or sister. An early study conducted by the University of Juba of children born in Juba, now considered the capital of South Sudan, notes just such a practice, though with a disparaging spin: "The most harmful social condition for the babies is the practice of mothers going to work or market for most of the day and leaving their babies in the care of an older child. When we visited the homes of marasmic or less severely malnourished children the mothers were almost invariably absent and the babies in the care of older children often no more than 7–8 years old."[16] This is not, however, unusual in African culture in general and serves as practical training for a future role in motherhood for young girls. A clinical psychologist and researcher in child development in Cameroon observes, "By means of practical training at different socially recognized life stages, children were increasingly integrated into the culture and community life through systematic incorporation into different interactions and role settings, particularly the caregiving culture, the domestic economy, and interpersonal encounters."[17]

15. These descriptions of family life and the traditions surrounding the birth of children were gleaned from numerous conversations with refugees from Sudan and from my observations of Dinka families at Kakuma Refugee Camp, Kenya, in 2003. Many of the childrearing practices have been somewhat modified because of the displacement experience.

16. Woodruff et al., "Infants," 506.

17. Nsamenang, "Early Childhood Care," 426.

The Dinka are a polygynous culture, and the role of co-wives is important to the network of care responsible for rearing of children. At about the age of one year, children are frequently sent to the nearby home of a co-wife so that weaning can be accomplished. If there are no co-wives, or they are too far away, the child may go to live with the grandmother for the duration of the weaning period. In fact, prior to the diaspora caused by war, the first child born to a Dinka mother was taken to live permanently (after the first year) with the maternal grandmother. This allowed the mother greater opportunity to conceive and bear a second child. The eldest child did not return to live with her or his birth family, though the child could visit as distance allowed. This may sound outrageous to many of us, but it often enhanced the possibility of maintaining the survival of offspring.

This communal participation in caring for children continues as they near adolescence but takes a slightly different form. Children move through this time in peer groups. Young boys will spend a great deal of time together tending cattle at "cattle camps" usually located some distance from home. In times past, these same peer groups eventually participated in rites of passage ushering them into manhood. Through this time, the male child is allowed into the company of nearly all male gatherings that include not only extended male family but other elders as well. Here the child listens to the stories of the ancestors, learns about politics and the responsibilities of a man to his family and community. A young girl begins to gather with other girls and then the women in a similar manner. She also learns stories about the ancestors, a female perspective on politics, and concerns in the community. These gatherings are of particular benefit to learning about childrearing and the other family-centered tasks of women.

Throughout childhood, the Dinka are exposed to an ever broadening sense of care and obligation within the community that moves from parent to stepfamilies to sibling caretakers to peer groups, to the community elders, and finally to the community of ancestors. It is the realm of spiritual healers and the sacred to which we now turn as we move deeper into understanding the moral obligation of care and healing within the community.

The Sacred Tradition of Spiritual Healing

A favorite tradition of the Dinka community, recalled by the Lost Boys, is storytelling around the fire.[18] At the close of the day, the elders gather with youngsters at their feet to tell and retell stories of history, lore, and tradition. Among these stories are those of the spiritual healers. Through centuries of war and subjugation, these healers have been responsible for tending to those who suffer.

The spread of Christianity had a devastating impact on the actual practices of spiritual healing among the Dinka. Early Christian missionaries demanded the surrender of any practices that could be interpreted as heretical. But limited medical alternatives made it difficult for the Dinka to completely abandon these practices. Today, especially in rural areas, Christianity is practiced in a form that has incorporated the best practices of both traditions.

Nevertheless, most of the Lost Boys and other Dinka I encountered had long ago forgone participation in these rituals of healing. But this seems to be an uneasy rejection of something so deeply held. The harder they push the ritual away, the more tightly they clutch the remnants left in memory. Deep threads continue to bind them to the healers of old. Emmanuel Lartey says of this powerful connection between the spirit world and the living world, "The Cosmos is inhabited and animated by numerous unseen forces, spirits, and gods, among which are the ancestral spirits—human spirits of departed members of the living human community. These forces have a crucial relationship with the physical and material forces of humanity and society."[19] These are forces not easily forfeited. One refugee made a poignant statement that reveals the depth of the conflict created by these threads: "Because I am a Christian, I cannot go there [to a healer]. I have to go to a doctor. I have to ask him [the healer] for advice, not to heal me." Clearly, abandonment of these practices is a choice imposed by the rules of

18. It is important to remember that these stories of the healing traditions were recalled by a group of young men who have had a significant interruption in the customary socialization process. Their memories of the rituals may, therefore, be incomplete or even idealized in certain ways that would appear contrary to accounts told by other children or even the elders themselves. This does not make them invalid, however. These are the memories and visions of Dinka tradition from which the Lost Boys drew as a resource in times of stress.

19. Lartey, "Globalization," 101.

Christianity, not a reflection on the efficacy, or lack thereof, of the ritual itself. And so, I look to these practices of healing not as alternatives for treating "symptoms" of PTSD or even a psychological interpretation of what healing means in the Dinka tradition. Rather, I consider the rituals of these healers as a backdrop against which to understand how, in the context of such a strong communal obligation of care and the devastating realities of war, the Lost Boys came to function, perhaps unconsciously, as a collective representation of the healers in ways that helped to lessen their own suffering.

Who the Healers Are and How to Find the Right One for the Job

While many in the Dinka culture will become elders, only a few are called to be healers. Most healers are born with a gift that becomes evident throughout childhood. Even some Lost Boys, having given up participation in healing rituals, still identify themselves in terms of the healer they would have been had they stayed in Sudan and not become a Christian. Whether one comes from a long line of healers or is the first in the family to show signs of the gift, the evidence of a special gift must be confirmed by the community of elders.

The elders—the most influential and powerful among the community—not only help discern who has been blessed with the gift of healing but also act as an important line of defense for anyone who is plagued by symptoms of physical or emotional distress. They comprise not the oldest members of the tribe but rather men and women who are thirty to fifty or sixty years old. Maturity is essential; even if marked with the gift of healing at a young age, one cannot officially function as a healer until being initiated as an elder.[20]

Just how one who was ill chose a healer was in many cases easy. While in our own culture we may start by seeing our general practitioner, when a member of the village became ill, he or she first consulted the healer most obviously suited to relieve the symptoms. If the illness or condition was not cured under the direction of that particular healer, then it was believed that a spiritual problem was underlying the physical one. In these cases the head elder, the *Alama*, in conjunction with the

20. There was some disagreement on this point that could not be completely reconciled. The majority of the refugees I talked to believed that indeed the healer must have the wisdom and status of an elder.

entire community of elders, acted as a referral center of sorts.[21] He was charged with knowing which spiritual healer, or *tiet*, was best suited to help that particular individual

The Healing Ritual

The healing ritual itself is very significant. When someone who is ill or in distress is directed to a spiritual healer, he or she consults the *tiet* in a special hut built just for this purpose. One refugee astutely notes that, at this point, the *tiet* acts much like a counselor by asking questions and, most important, listening to his patient. She or he is then told what has caused the illness and what must be done to address the problem. Instructions are given if an animal needs to be sacrificed for the benefit of an angry spirit, which usually takes place the following day along with the healing ceremony itself.

The physical positioning of each person at the healing ritual is very significant and describes a powerful vision of what becomes a "holding community." The healer, the one in distress along with her or his family, the elders, the general community, and a whole host of ancestors are included in the ceremony. The healer is stationed at one end of the space with no one sitting behind him or her.[22] In front of him or her are

21. Also of great importance to the cultural practices of the Dinka are the ancestor spirits. Upon death the spirit was thought to ascend to a place called in some stories *the place of the living dead*. When asked if this is a good or a bad place the Lost Boys replied that each person will experience it according to how they have lived their life. Nevertheless all will go to the same place. Each family member that has died and now resides in the spirit world is an ancestor spirit. Ancestors may return through dreams or intervene in everyday life to offer help. According to the interview group, an ancestor will rarely be a source of harm.

The Dinka vision of the cosmos is not three tiered as in some cultures. When asked if there is an underworld or someplace that is home to evil spirits, the young men replied, no. There seems to be an understanding that there are only two realms: this world of the fleshly body and the heavenly world of the spirit. Evil, assigned to the realm of an underworld by some cultures including the West, is considered to be possible among all spirits. Good and evil are equal possibilities in each person and each spirit. Likewise, the soul cannot be taken from an individual or lost by some evil means. A spirit may afflict its victim, may cause pain or illness, but the soul itself is not under threat of annihilation. This may have interesting implications for our understanding of how the *tiet*, or spiritual healer, functions among the Dinka.

22. The *tiet* will perform various functions to begin the ritual, such as rubbing the upper torso of the suffering person's body with some element in preparation for the ritual. Most often a *kuol jok*, or kiwi fruit believed to be blessed by God because of its

two rows of people sitting parallel to and facing one another. In one row is the family of the one in distress; facing them are the elders. Between the two parallel rows, facing the healer, sits the one who awaits healing. The general community surrounds them all. *Healing always takes place in the context of community.*

The gathered community plays the drums and sings to entreat the necessary ancestor or spirit. This song typically tells the story of a brave act or good deed for which that ancestor is remembered. At this point, the *tiet* enters the realm of the spirits. Healers are not known to ingest any particular substance to facilitate this state, but it is accompanied by the deep beating of the drum. Anthropologist Holger Kalweit suggests that the deep percussion rhythm of continuous beating can serve to transition one into an altered state of consciousness. He says, "Rhythm and consciousness are intimately bound up together. An alteration of our bodily rhythms creates a change in our consciousness."[23] Several of the Lost Boys recall that as the ceremony progresses, the healer's face often becomes distorted and he/she makes strange physical motions. This is usually accompanied by strange sounds and the speaking of some unknown language. The Lost Boys understand these behaviors to mark the moment when the healer begins speaking to his/her helping spirit, who subsequently confronts the offending spirit. This ecstatic display can result in a high level of agitation as the spirits argue with each other over the state of the "patient." When the *tiet* eventually returns to this realm, he/she translates the events and reveals what the spirits said.

The ceremony closes as the community again sings to the ancestor but this time bidding him or her goodbye. A thankful family may pay the healer for time and energy with a cow or other animal. On occasion a *tiet* refuses payment, feeling instead that he/she is obligated to share the gift of healing without compensation. [24]

---

abundance, is cut in two equal halves, and then applied to the individual. Some *tiet* will read or interpret the seeds of the fruit to discern necessary information. Sometimes the blood (from the sacrificed animal), ashes, oil, or water may also be used.

23. Kalweit, *Shamans*, 84–85.

24. On occasion the *tiet* reaches the limits of his abilities and does not heal the individual. In such a case the one in distress seeks the additional services of another *tiet*.

The Function of the *Tiet* in the Dinka Community

How does the *tiet* serve the social, psychological, and religious needs of the Dinka community? Socially, the *tiet* acts as spokesperson simultaneously for the community of Dinka and for the community of spirits. As spokesperson, he or she is charged with bearing witness to, defining justice for, and accompanying the afflicted through illness and suffering. As witness, the *tiet* sees into the depths of suffering and pain. He or she likewise seeks to restore the life of the afflicted with a just balance between body and spirit. Finally, it is only the *tiet* who dares enter into the physical or emotional illness itself and accompany the victim into the midst of the suffering. As a representative of the entire family of Dinka, the *tiet* becomes the embodiment of the whole. As such, he or she is the strongest thread that binds together the healing process.

This dependence upon the community remains crucial even for Dinka in the United States. It has been a very difficult transition to the individualistic American culture. While the young men understand the benefits of medicine and technology, our culture expects them to carry the burden of suffering quietly and privately. This is especially true in the area of mental health. The demand to think in terms of an individual (psychotherapy) and to withhold information about oneself from others (confidentiality) is contrary to all that these young men know as part of the Dinka community. Not to share one's pain is an indication, a refugee says, that you do not trust your family.

The most powerful image of the *tiet* is that of *the one who speaks*. To the one who suffers the *tiet* brings order and power in the act of naming.[25] As one charged with accompanying those afflicted with illness, the *tiet* must move into the upside-down world of the spirits. This is a chaotic world that often mirrors the inner turmoil of one who suffers. The *tiet*'s ability to name the illness and the spirit responsible for it begins the process of bringing order to the pain and relief from emotional suffering. Likewise, to feel one's body in the throes of illness, even if it is in defense against that which is attacking it, but not be able to control the suffering is a primal form of helplessness. When the *tiet*

25. Rapinski-Naxon notes Levi-Strauss's analysis that the shaman speaks while the psychoanalyst listens. Naxon summarizes the thought: "[the shaman] affords his client a language that provides an instant outlet for mental and psychic states that otherwise could remain buried within or incapable of finding expression" (Ripinsky-Naxon, *The Nature of Shamanism*, 102).

confronts the spirits and speaks on behalf of the victim, the *tiet* restores a sense of power to the one who suffers.

The Lost Boys astutely identified the ability of the *tiet* to listen to and talk with the victim as characteristic of our modern-day counselor. This seems very appropriate. Many Western diagnostic tools are, as we saw in chapter 4, very quick to name mental illness, including posttraumatic stress disorder. And yet, mental health professionals using common forms of "talk therapy" are reluctant to speak as assertively as the *tiet* to define the nature of the problem at hand. Rather, therapists often feel it to be a more ethical practice to guide a client and allow individuals to discover for themselves the answers to their own questions. For the Dinka, this approach makes little sense. For a doctor, psychologist, or pastoral counselor not to tell the patient what is wrong and how to repair it leaves the patient powerless, without a voice, and, as one refugee stated, without a healer. This creates an interesting conflict when Western diagnostic or treatment methods do not take cultural context into consideration.

Most important, it is the *tiet*'s intimate connection with the holy that makes healing a sacred act and brings the community into the presence of the sacred, none of which can be separated from the other. When the *tiet* transcends this world and stands in the presence of the sacred as the embodiment of the Dinka community, he or she ushers the community into that space. In spite of the emergence of Christianity in the Dinka community, this religious function of the *tiet* has maintained its importance. It is precisely this ability to create a sacred space for healing that nurtures the continued longing for the presence of the *tiet*—even to this day.

Creating a Relatively Safe Holding Place

One outgrowth of the communal obligation just described lies in the impulse to create a safe holding place for the community much like the one created by the spiritual healer or the ritual itself. Ideally speaking, a safe place is one free of violence or threat. Indeed, Judith Herman sees this as fundamental to healing from traumatic experience.[26] In times of war and prolonged displacement, this kind of safety is not a reasonable

26. Herman, *Trauma and Recovery*.

option. Does this mean there is no way to minimize the sense of vulnerability and subsequent helplessness? To the contrary, I suggest that the Lost Boys created a relatively safe holding place. What do I mean by a relatively safe holding place? *Relative safety*, in this use, means to lessen danger through cooperative participation. Certainly there is no possibility of a group of children creating a completely safe space in the middle of war. But the Lost Boys have demonstrated that together they found ways to reduce the danger, even if minimally, in certain situations. By *holding place*, I am suggesting the characteristics found in the intersubjective space of the therapeutic environment, if only in effect. In other words, I mean a temporary psychic space, and when possible a physical space, created between individuals (or a group) out of mutual belief and trust, the result of which is of positive psychological benefit.[27]

Judith Herman proposes that healing from PTSD includes three phases. The first and perhaps most important of the three is establishing safety. A victim of trauma must establish safety or control of his or her body, then over the environment. Herman writes:

> Establishing safety begins by focusing on control of the body and gradually moves outward toward control of the environment. Issues of bodily integrity include attention to basic health needs, regulation of bodily functions such as sleep, eating, and exercise, management of post-traumatic symptoms, and control of self-destructive behaviors. Environmental issues include the

27. I note here Winnicott's use of potential space, that is, the hypothetical space between mother and child and the mother's holding function that in the best of circumstances offers a degree of safety in the midst of psychological danger at the time of separation from which the child may emerge as a more autonomous self. The significance of potential space, as well as the holding function of the therapist, reemerges during the therapeutic encounter. Winnicott says, "This is exactly the same as the danger area that is arrived at sooner or later in all psychiatric treatments, the patient having felt secure and viable because of the analyst's reliability, adaptation to need, and willingness to become involved, and now beginning to feel a need to shake free and to achieve autonomy. Like the baby with the mother, the patient cannot become autonomous except in conjunction with the therapist's readiness to let go, and yet any move on the part of the therapist away from a state of being merged in with the patient is under dire suspicion, so that disaster threatens" (Winnicott, *Playing*, 107). This idea of a holding environment in the face of danger, in addition to Edward Farley's understanding of the community's role in naming "a people's shared way of understanding the places that are safe," has influenced my use of the term *relatively safe holding place* (Farley, *Good and Evil*, 53).

establishment of a safe living situation, financial security, mobility, and a plan for self-protection that encompasses the full
range of the patient's daily life. Because no one can establish
a safe environment alone, the task of developing an adequate
safety plan always includes a component of social support.[28]

Clearly, this level of bodily or environmental safety is not possible
while fleeing war or even in the refugee camp. But in the midst of such
volatile circumstances, even relative efforts at safety and control can
have a powerful effect. Consider the story of how the elder Lost Boys
encircled the younger ones while fighting off lions; or, using that same
method, how the elders surrounded the youngsters as they slept under
the tent in the refugee camp. Even though the younger Lost Boys were
very afraid, they were not left to fend for themselves, helpless and alone.
Always there was a community of older brothers who tried to keep them
safe. The elder boys for whom the threat was increased as they tried to
protect the younger ones were empowered by the act of honoring their
obligation to care for their brothers.

When the Lost Boys arrived at Kakuma, they were able to sustain
this supportive and nurturing community by living together in small
groups (four or more) in dorm-type living huts. Even though, by then,
they had at least some adult supervision, the boys continued to take care
of each other. This Dinka manner of negotiating the world as a community was perhaps the single-most unique aspect of the Lost Boys that
we experienced as a resettlement agency. They were given the option by
the government to resettle in "family groups" and arrived off the plane
in these groups. Once in Nashville, the resettlement agency continued
to honor these family groups by housing them together in apartments,
with the other Lost Boys living nearby. Quickly, acquaintances were
found and new groups of elders took charge of managing such things
as discipline and acting as spokespersons in negotiating injustices. Even
in this new environment, elder Lost Boys continued to surround and
protect the younger or less able, thus helping to manage postmigration
stress more effectively.

Research is now revealing the negative effects on Lost Boys of
not being able to live in a community of Dinka brothers. Geltman et
al. suggest the following: "Children [Lost Boys] who were living alone

28. Herman, *Trauma and Recovery*, 160.

in foster care with an American family or in a group home felt more isolated . . . and were also more likely to have PTSD and lower CHQ [Child Health Questionnaire] scores. This suggests that relative levels of family and community engagement after arriving in the United States may mediate the ultimate impact of early trauma on later psychosocial functioning."[29] This research does not consider the deep communal traditions that undergird the Dinka upbringing, and thus we are left to speculate on whether it is individual factors or the home placements themselves that increase symptoms of PTSD.

The Lost Boys defied the great sense of disconnect that victims of violence so often feel. Herman describes it this way: "Traumatized people feel utterly abandoned, utterly alone, cast out of the human and divine systems of care and protection that sustain life. Thereafter, a sense of alienation, of disconnection, pervades every relationship, from the most intimate familial bonds to the most abstract affiliations of community and religion. When trust is lost, traumatized people feel that they belong more to the dead than to the living."[30] The Lost Boys managed to mitigate this experience and maintain their connection to each other in very overt and sometimes in very subtle ways.

Articulating Justice

The Lost Boys also learned the importance of creating the voice of justice within the community. Like the healer who argues for and demands justice for the one who suffers, the Lost Boys learned to articulate the injustices and demand reparations for the moral injury. Clearly this too must be understood in relative terms. This small community of refugees could not change the course of the war because of their calls for justice. There is a powerful effect, however, that comes when the traumatically injured are surrounded by a community that names the wrong and demands justice. Judith Herman makes a strong claim for the role of the community and justice in facilitating healing from PTSD. She writes, "The response of the community has a powerful influence on the ultimate resolution of the trauma. Restoration of the breach between the traumatized person and the community depends, first, upon public acknowledgment of the traumatic event and, second, upon some form

29. Geltman et al., "The 'Lost Boys of Sudan,'" 589.

30. Herman, *Trauma and Recovery*, 52.

of community action. Once it is publicly recognized that a person has been harmed, the community must take action to assign responsibility for the harm and to repair the injury. These two responses—recognition and restitution—are necessary to rebuild the survivor's sense of order and justice."[31] We can see here that Herman is speaking of community in the context of the larger society (e.g., the damaging effect of the general public's opposition during the Vietnam War) that defines what is just. Nonetheless, she seems to describe the positive actions of the Lost Boys who negotiated the stresses of life in the refugee camp and the resettlement process in just this manner.

For resettlement workers, it was a dreaded sight to see a delegation of Lost Boys walking down the hallway toward our office. We grew to recognize the stern set jaws and determined but mostly polite attitudes of elders who came to negotiate a perceived injustice. In the beginning days, the meetings usually centered on the disturbing fact that one refugee apartment had been supplied with something that the others had not. For example, volunteers had given a VCR to the household for which they were responsible. Others did not have a VCR. By analogy, the story of the car told earlier in the chapter makes it easy to locate the injustice in this example. Indeed, a delegation arrived at our office to discuss the problem: one household has something that the others do not. In the context of American culture, the injustices seem slight or even nonexistent. To the Lost Boys the injustice was unacceptable. Similar discussions were held when the medicine prescribed by a doctor failed to heal a refugee of his particular ailment. This was seen as an injustice that needed rectification.

In Kakuma Refugee Camp I was met by more than one of these delegations. Their intent was to tell me about the lack of food, the lack of safety, the deplorable living conditions, and the need for education among other things. These problems were, and are, moral issues. The Lost Boys understood that humans should not live this way and expected something to be done about it.

Creating a Collective Trauma Story

From the traditions of the *tiet* the community of Lost Boys learned about the power and even the necessity of giving voice to suffering.

31. Ibid., 70.

Through the trials of their journey, the refugee camp, and finally resettlement in the United States (as described in chapter 2), the Lost Boys have committed themselves to giving voice to a collective trauma narrative. The upside-down, chaotic world of the one who suffers, like the one negotiated by the *tiet*, speaks fittingly of the world characterized by traumatic experience. While Western talk therapy demands a focus on the individual experience for narrative to be beneficial, the Lost Boys are bound to the communal experience. By collectively giving voice to their experience, they not only enter into the suffering together but out of its depths bring new meaning, incorporated into the larger Dinka story. Janice Goodman remarks about this in her research with the Lost Boys: "Each participant located himself predominantly as part of the group of refugee boys, telling his story with the group voice, mainly using the pronouns *we* and *us*, and only rarely using the personal pronouns *I* or *me*. A sense of shared experience and collective coping enabled survival."[32]

In the refugee camp, the collective trauma story attracted the attention of the government officials, who eventually declared the Lost Boys a special population eligible for resettlement in the United States. Ten years after being christened with the name *Lost Boys*, key aspects of the collective story of suffering and escape became the literal criteria for acceptance as one of the "unaccompanied minors" being resettled in the United States.

Once the Lost Boys began arriving in the United States, the collective story of the Lost Boys grew to mythic proportions. Many, especially longtime supporters of the Lost Boys, might take offense at my categorizing their story as a myth, perhaps believing I am implying that it is a fabrication. But such is not the case. I recall a true-or-false question on a college exam many years ago: a myth is an important way of telling the truth. Indeed the Lost Boys have found a very important way of telling a truth larger than any single experience of suffering—a collective trauma story that honors the Dinka notion that the individual emerges only as a part of the collective and binds individuals in a community of shared experience.

Their collective story helped bring notoriety to the Lost Boys, though this was at times unhelpful. Some volunteers, galvanized by the

32. Goodman, "Coping with Trauma," 1183.

heartbreaking story of suffering, wanted to adopt the young men, now adults, as though they were still small children in need of protection. The news media could not get enough of the stories of suffering and perseverance, particularly after the young men started, against all odds, to excel, especially in education. While the collective trauma story framed them as a target of sympathy, affection, and philanthropy, the Lost Boys themselves, driven by the tradition of the healing narratives of old, pushed on toward a deeper meaning for themselves and their people. It is this same collective trauma story that the Dinka would come to believe tells of how God works to bring peace to South Sudan.

Summary

Early in my research with the Lost Boys, I encountered an article by Martin Teicher that proposes the possibility that the stress of violence, abuse, or neglect experienced by children can cause "electrical irritability" in the brain, which literally reshapes certain areas.[33] Though adaptive as an evolutionary strategy, these changes leave lasting negative psychological effects in adulthood. Teicher states, "Whether it comes in the form of physical, emotional or sexual trauma or through exposure to warfare, famine or pestilence, stress can set off a ripple of hormonal changes that permanently wire a child's brain to cope with a malevolent world."[34] As I read this article in light of what I knew about the Lost Boy community, I could not help but ask the question: Would a surrounding community (though itself facing violence) that provided care and relative safety have a mitigating effect on these electrical impulses? Could the community, in fact, lessen the negative impact on the brain? This is the very question that led me to examine the ways that the Lost Boys functioned to lessen the long-term negative psychological effects of their traumatic experiences.

I have suggested that the traditions of childrearing create a network of empathetic caregivers who help create internal structures of the Dinka self that are strongest when one's care and obligation to the community are honored. This in turn has led the Lost Boys to care for each other during their flight from war, in the refugee camps, and as

33. Teicher, "Scars," 68–75.
34. Ibid., 75.

they resettled in the United States in a manner that re-created familial and tribal structures of support. Elder boys took responsibility for protecting, disciplining, and providing physical care for the younger boys. Thus, pseudofamily systems among the "brothers" replaced family structures that had been ripped apart by the displacement.

The Lost Boys intuitively functioned much like the healers of past Dinka tradition to articulate justice for one another in their suffering and to express a collective trauma narrative that bound each to the other in their suffering. The stories recounted around the campfire taught the boys how the healers argued with the spirits on behalf of those in distress and told the story of or became the voice for those who suffer. They incorporated these functions into the bedrock of care and obligations expected of each other. The story of suffering for one became the story of suffering for all. This collective trauma narrative incorporates all their stories and attempts to bring meaning to their experience by putting it in the context of the greater Dinka narrative. In the midst of their own upside-down world, in which justice had no frame, they created their own healing space based upon the rules of care and obligation taught in the earliest of years. The function of this justice is seen not in its effectiveness to move or change the larger society but in its ability to provide a moral frame in the midst of unspeakable injustice. Though this may have little power to obtain restitution in the broader sense, it lessens the likelihood that many Lost Boys will be left to question their own culpability for the tragedy that has befallen them.

Finally, the community of Lost Boys functioned to provide a relatively safe holding place for one another in the midst of constant threat. Sometimes this relatively safe place was at the center of a circle of elder brothers who were fighting off lions or other threats. There was unquestionably great fear, even terror; yet as long as the younger boys stayed in this circle, they were not left to feel helpless in fending for themselves. Such action allowed the Lost Boys to travel through volatile areas depending upon each to the other for support and comfort that, in the end, empowered them in the most difficult of circumstances.

The Lost Boy community's ability to mitigate the symptoms of traumatic stress is grounded in the life-sustaining obligation of care toward each other. It is a community through which many can learn, including the scientific community—who, while earnestly seeking to help those suffering the effects of traumatic experience due to war and violence, often overlooks the valuable impact of deeply set cultural traditions that have their own power of healing. Among these cultural traditions, a religious worldview may prove one of the most powerful forces for resilience.

6

A Communal Faith Narrative

Our hope comes from God.

—Refugee from Bor, Sudan

THE DINKA LIVE WITH AN IMPULSE TOWARD STORY. AS WE have seen, stories of the great spiritual healers serve to remind the Dinka of the power of community and bind them to ancestors throughout history.[1] Many generations ago, this connection itself was the source of healing in times of distress. Today, biblical stories inspire the Dinka to remember God's promise of redemption even under the most extreme circumstances. Spiritual and other healing practices have been replaced in large measure by devoted prayer to Jesus. In spite of Western medicine, which is used when available and affordable, it is Jesus whom the Dinka see as the great healer.

Even though the actual practices are no longer used by most Dinka, the tradition of the spiritual healers is embedded in the Lost Boys; and from these practices, they have learned to embrace certain pillars of resilience that have helped mitigate the effects of their many traumatic experiences. But as we listen to the Dinka, we discover that the roots of these practices lie not only in long-held community tradition but also in their Christian faith. The acts of naming justice, creating safe

1. Portions of this chapter were first published in the *Journal for Pastoral Theology* 20 (2010) and are reprinted here with permission.

space, and telling a collective trauma story find their ultimate fulfillment only in the context of a larger story—a Christian faith narrative. I
propose that by living into this faith narrative, through which they are
active participants in the unfolding of God's promise of redemption,
the Dinka community attempts to make sense of their suffering and are
empowered to lay claim to a valuable source of resilience in the midst
of traumatic experience.

Narrative and Future Story

Andrew Lester in his wonderful book *Hope in Pastoral Care and
Counseling* addresses the power of story, or narrative, to indicate an individual's ability to negotiate hope. In particular, he points to the ability
to construct what he calls a *functional* future story as being a key indicator of one's capacity to hope in a given circumstance.[2] A functional
future story incorporates the reality of a situation but moves forward
into an open-ended future nurtured by possibility. This is, of course, the
idyllic vision of a functional future story; and in times of crisis, most
of us will, until the sharpest pains begin to dull, manage only to sput-
ter toward it. But Lester notes that for many, it is the sacred stories of
our faith tradition that help us make a shift in our own stories toward
a sense of hope.[3] These sacred stories help us to remember that our
personal stories are set in the context of a God who is larger than our
own reality. For Lester, it is this transfinite hope that sets the frame for
our finite hopes.[4]

Even though most of Lester's case studies focus on individuals, he
is clear that future stories and, ultimately, hope are always set in the
context of community. Core narratives, how we explain our world and
our place in it, develop in the context of family, neighborhood, faith
community, and culture.[5] I suggest that communal future stories, particularly faith narratives, are essential in influencing how communities
of faith envision hope in times of trauma. A communal faith narrative
is a story told by the community itself of how God works through that
group to make God's unfolding promise a reality. Such faith narratives

2. Lester, *Hope in Pastoral Care*, 94.

3. Ibid., 39.

4. Ibid., 65.

5. Ibid., 30, 37.

are deeply embedded in the culture and ethos of a community. Just as in the case of individual future stories, uncovering the faith narrative of a community can provide insights into its health and capacity for hope. Even a community searching for a God who seems hidden still has a faith narrative to tell, albeit a painful one. Ultimately, a community's ability to see their own role in the story of God in the world, especially in times of tragedy, provides a deep well of resilience that fosters hope and may help mitigate the damaging effects of trauma.

Sacred Stories

Blessed are the poor in spirit, for theirs is the kingdom of heaven.
Blessed are those who mourn, for they will be comforted.
Blessed are the meek, for they will inherit the earth.
Blessed are those who hunger and thirst for righteousness, for they will be filled.
Blessed are the merciful, for they will receive mercy.
Blessed are the pure in heart, for they will see God.
Blessed are the peacemakers, for they will be called children of God.
Blessed are those who are persecuted for righteousness's sake for theirs is the kingdom of heaven.
Blessed are you when people revile you and persecute you and utter all kinds of evil against you falsely on my account. Rejoice and be glad, for your reward is great in heaven, for in the same way they persecuted the prophets who were before you.

—Matthew 5:1–12 (NRSV), a frequent "anchor Scripture" in Bor

As Lester suggests, sacred stories have a powerful impact on our own narratives. In the case of the Dinka, sacred stories in the form of biblical Scripture help fortify and shape their faith narrative even as they actively live into its promise. The Dinka relationship to the Bible is influenced by its missionary roots and bears a rich evangelical flavor. Fewer than 15 percent of the pastors in the vicinity of Bor in the south of Sudan have any theological training. Interpretation of Scripture is not an emotionally removed intellectual pursuit; rather, it is raw, visceral, and quite personal. Scripture sustains the Dinka in two primary ways: through the use of what I have called *anchor Scriptures* and as a frame for understanding their own experiences of suffering that connects them to the larger Christian narrative, particularly ancient Israel.

Anchor Scriptures are biblical passages relied upon for comfort and strength during difficult times and are exchanged in daily interactions with one another. These passages are beloved companions that have been well tested over time, which, like anchors, have helped individuals, families, or communities secure themselves against the daily onslaught of suffering. As the Word of God, these Scriptures hold the tangible power to provide strength in the face of adversity and despair. During my time in Kakuma and Bor, it was common, whether meeting with an individual or group, to be given an offering of an anchor Scripture.

Sometimes the Scripture was read in Dinka, at other times a passage was paraphrased from memory, and at still other times the mere mention of the book and chapter would suffice. The choice of delivery method was often a pragmatic one; many Dinka were not literate, and fewer still owned Bibles from which to read. The sharing of anchor Scriptures was not a form of proof-texting. Rather, it generally preceded the sharing of concerns or confession of suffering. Though the verses of an anchor Scripture were often delivered from memory, this practice was not the same as a Bible drill or *sword drill*, as it is known to my Baptist colleagues: that is, the recitation of Scripture to help children learn the location of Bible passages. What they do have in common, though, is the ultimate goal that memorized Scripture be, as British Baptist theologian Derek Tidball says, "a means of letting the Bible's words become a deep part of one's being, of sinking into one's mind and becoming the default mechanism by which one thought and acted."[6]

I interpret the offering of these anchor Scriptures as a combination of *greeting, prayer,* and *gift* all rolled into one. As greeting, anchor Scriptures framed our human encounters, which took place in sometimes very meager surroundings among those for whom life was visibly a daily struggle. Such greetings served as a call of gathering that invited God's presence. This was a particularly important part of communal gatherings. Anchor Scriptures were always incorporated into public events, including community and church meetings as well as feasts and celebrations. The fact that an assigned elder at a meeting opened the gathering with a particular Scripture did not preclude another elder

6. Tidball, "The Bible and Evangelical Spirituality," 267.

from offering their own anchor Scripture when it became her or his turn to speak.

As prayer, these scriptural offerings wove lament, supplication, and thanksgiving together in ways that survivors of other disasters may recognize. It was common to hear in the same breath a deep gratitude for peace, even a relative one; the unending grief over parents and children killed or lost; and the plea for sustenance when there was no food to fill empty bellies. The range of sometimes conflicting emotional and spiritual needs was very wide indeed. Sharing the Word was a prayerful reminder that God brings us to this day and this place whether it be to struggle or celebrate.

Even before I understood the intention behind anchor Scriptures, I was nonetheless quite certain that 'thank you' was the appropriate response. As gift, the Word is intended to uplift and fortify the recipient by assuring one of the bold promise of a faithful God who carries us into the future, even an uncertain one. Each offering was generously shared not only with the intention that I be blessed with the same comfort they had experienced but also with the expectation that I would go on to share it with others.

Whether such an offering served as greeting, prayer, or gift, there was a clear ethical dimension underlying the choice of anchor Scriptures I encountered. For example, I frequently received passages that included James 4 ("Draw near to God and he will draw near to you"); Psalm 15 ("O Lord, who may abide in your tent? Those who walk blamelessly and do what is right"); and Matthew 5, commonly called the Beatitudes. Matthew 5 is a fundamentally important text in this community and was referred to far more than any other biblical passage. Indeed, to the Dinka, the blessings in the beatitudes not only point toward a vision of what God's salvation will look like but also help frame right conduct, which is especially important in times of violence and destruction. This and other anchor Scriptures help reinforce the moral obligation of care that is so profoundly essential to the resilience of Dinka people. For this community, right conduct and that which is most pleasing to God are the very things most threatened by displacement and war.

Anchor Scriptures also create a powerful link to spiritual ancestors of the Bible and place Dinka suffering within the larger Christian narrative. This healing connection to God through spiritual ancestors has, in large measure, replaced a reliance on Dinka legends and ancestor songs; the latter were used to invoke the power of the ancestors and usher the sacred into the community. Ancestor songs, sung long ago by the community to bring forth a particular ancestor during a healing ritual, are another example. These simple songs told the story of that ancestor's hunting prowess, acts of bravery, or good deeds and often reflected their wisdom and respect for the sacred. Ancestors had the power to speak directly to the sacred on behalf of the living. Through these beckoning songs, spiritual healers and ancestors joined together with the community on behalf of one who suffered to bring healing and peace. Most important, they brought the individual story of suffering into relationship with the whole narrative of the community, both living and dead. During the war, many Dinka came to believe that by holding on to these old stories and traditional healing practices, they were being unfaithful to God. As the Dinka came to rely more on Jesus Christ as the ultimate healer and Savior, they let go of the old ways and held tightly to their anchor Scriptures that bound them, and the whole Dinka community, to their biblical ancestors within the larger Christian narrative.

A Faith Narrative Unfolding

When trying to understand the unimaginable—traumatic events such as war, loss, and displacement—the Dinka look back to their biblical ancestors as they grasp for meaning. Here, they find a model in ancient Israel, who understood the horrors of war, loss of loved ones, and expulsion from their beloved land. Within this biblical narrative, the Dinka see a faithful God who would not forsake them, as well as a story of accountability for their own future. Thus, I have framed the Dinka faith narrative in three parts: (1) Exile, where the Dinka look back on their experience of fleeing war and living in a refugee camp; (2) the Remnant, describing a group of children who survived the long trek across Sudan unaccompanied by adults and were later singled out for resettlement in the West; and (3) Redemption, which describes God's working through the remnant to bring peace and development to South Sudan. With God's promise laid out before them, the Dinka people are empowered with a sense of purpose and agency that pushes against the helplessness so often felt by victims of war and trauma, and moves them toward meaning making.

Exile

War came because we were not righteous . . . God brought this war so that those who didn't know God would know Him. We praised Him in our difficult times before the peace was signed, and that is why we are here at this time. He heard our prayers.

—Refugee from Bor

By the time the war began, most of the Dinka had been Christians for decades. Initially, Christianity, in the eyes of many Dinka, was seen as largely compatible with their traditional beliefs. This was especially true in rural areas and remains true even today. Ancestors and other deities continued to be considered as quite significant. In Dinka tradition, the hierarchy of deities included a supreme God known as *Nhialic*, which means "the creator God."[7] The belief that the Christian God incorporated the supreme god, Nhialic, as well as all the lesser gods of the Dinka tradition made it an easy shift in thought for many who converted to Christianity but also allowed for a merging of beliefs in a way that maintained the use of spiritual healing and sorcery. African theologian John Mbiti proposes that, in fact, there is no division between the creator God of indigenous communities and the Christian God when he says,

> The God described in the Bible is none other than the God who is already known in the framework of our traditional African religiosity. The missionaries who introduced the gospel to Africa in the past two hundred years did not bring God to our continent. Instead, God brought *them*. They proclaimed the name of Jesus Christ. But they used the names of the God who was and is already known by African peoples—such as Mungu, Mulungu, Katonda . . . and a thousand more. These were not empty names. They were names of one and the same God, the creator of the world, the father of our Lord Jesus Christ.[8]

Nonetheless, in the eyes of many Dinka this merging of beliefs forestalled what, after years in the refugee camps exposed to a more rigid

7. The supreme god was known by many names, including *Dichiek* and *Achiek*—though *Nhailic* remained most popular, according to the refugees. Interestingly, Nhialic's power to create was so respected that, like the Hebrew language of the Old Testament, the Dinka language has no word meaning "to create" that can be used in reference to a human subject. The Dinka believe that only God (Nhialic) can create; human beings can make, do, form, etc., but not create.

8. Mbiti, "The Encounter," 201.

form of missionary Christianity, they came to understand as a complete conversion to Jesus Christ as healer and Savior. The Dinka continue to struggle with this sense of unfaithfulness within the community as the old practices still flourish in certain remote areas of Sudan.

As we have already seen, before the civil war in South Sudan, the Dinka maintained a pastoral existence and supplemented this with some agriculture. Men tended to cattle, an essential indicator of prosperity and the predominate currency for what they call a dowry.[9] As the war progressed, millions fled to Kakuma Refugee Camp in the desert of northern Kenya. Here, grazing cattle and the idea of growing corn beside the Nile became a treasured but distant memory. As refugees, they lived in cramped, dusty compounds and were not allowed to own animals even if they had money. The brutal sun, lack of space, and rationing of water made it nearly impossible for crops to survive. During my visit to Kakuma in 2003, I recorded this field note describing what had become their place of exile:

> Here in Kakuma, the heat is brutal. Each breeze carries only swirling dust and little relief. . . The grit of the dust and the smells of human waste are overwhelming . . . Food rations were given yesterday—lines of children and adults whose stomachs have not known food for days. The portions of raw grains are meager but intended to last two weeks. Refugees say they will only last five days. Medicine is limited. Fourteen textbooks must be shared by 120 students. Water is rationed. There is not enough to drink, cook, and bathe. One must choose. To come now to this dry and desolate place seems to hold a grief all its own.

Perhaps surprisingly, the civil war marked a period of spiritual formation unlike any other in the lives of the Dinka people. Faith became a lifeline to hope, and exposure to the missionary Christianity of the refugee camps highlighted the need to leave behind traditional beliefs in favor of a complete commitment to Christ. The Dinka came to understand the recent war, as with all things, to have been under the control of God's divine power. The war was God's punishment for not living

---

9. The practice of the groom's or the groom's family's offering goods to the bride's family is typically referred to as *brideprice* or *bridewealth*, though the Dinka translate it as *dowry*. Used outside of this context a dowry usually denotes the practice of the bride's family offering goods or money to the groom's family (Anderson, "The Economics of Dowry," 152).

faithfully. The Dinka believe that to return to God's blessing, they must endure the hardships before them and above all be faithful because the day will come when God will save them. This longing for God's forgiveness and the need to maintain the community's moral obligation of care strengthened their reliance on Scripture. The development of the faith narrative that we consider here occurred over a long process of weaving the Dinka story of loss and suffering with that of their spiritual ancestors in ancient Israel, and points not just toward a caring God but to their full redemption through Jesus Christ.

The Remnant

If we can keep them [the children] alive through this horrible time in Kakuma, if they have a chance at education—then Sudan will live. That is our hope.

—Dinka elder, Kakuma Refugee Camp, Kenya

Perhaps every generation in every place has, to some degree, defined its greatest blessing by its children. But blessing in the life of a refugee requires negotiating when to hold fast to what is most dear, and when to surrender it to greater possibility. This is the paradoxical bind the Dinka found themselves in with regard to their children in Kakuma. On the one hand, they invested all means available, meager though they may have been, to find and reunite with lost children, to nurture and sustain those they had, and to create new life when possible. After so many years of war and so much death, the practical need to replenish families was ongoing.

On the other hand, the Dinka were also faced with the gut-wrenching decision to, as they describe it, "give their children to America." By this they meant sending a remnant of their children, namely, the Lost Boys, to the United States for resettlement. In doing so, the Dinka faced the real possibility that they would never see their children again but also the possibility that through these children, like the remnant of Israel, South Sudan would survive.

These children were the Lost Boys. By 1999 many had grown into young men and gained the attention of the International Office of Migration. They were designated a "special population," which gave a small number the opportunity to resettle in another country. The clans, sensing the monumental implications for what lay ahead in the lives of these young men, prepared them for the arduous journey before them. As the young men tell it, when word was received of a youngster's departure date from Kakuma, the elders prepared a feast and invited the community to gather. The elders instructed him on his obligations to God, his education, and the community. The Lost Boys left for America in the full realization that the Dinka community expected them to live toward the future of Sudan.

By the summer of 2001, slightly less than four thousand Lost Boys (and a few hundred Lost Girls) had been resettled in the United States. Their heart-wrenching story of survival and incredible resilience won the hearts of thousands of Americans who heard it. Especially because they were known to be devoted Christians, many church congregations committed themselves to helping these young men adapt to their new lives. With the near halt of refugee admittances to the United States after the events of September 11, thousands of Lost Boys and other refugees remaining in the camp lost their chance to find a new home in the United States.

Redemption

Those who went to America are our hope from God—we have handed over their lives to God . . . Our peace came from God and our children who went to America. It is all His work.

—Refugee from Bor

The Lost Boys have received so much attention in this country that it is easy to forget that they are only a part of a much larger narrative among the Dinka people. The signing of the Comprehensive Peace Agreement in 2005, which suspended the hostilities between the government forces from the North and the Sudan People's Liberation Movement/Army (SPLM/A) in the South, is foundational to the Dinka belief that God is working through the Lost Boys to bring literal and spiritual salvation to a hurting people. A woman elder from Bor said that the Dinka, including the Lost Boys themselves, see the peace agreement as a tangible sign of God working through these young men. One of the Lost Boys explained, "We tried many times but not until they [the Lost Boys] came to the U.S. and got everyone's attention did peace come . . .

God worked through the Lost Boys to get America to stop the war." The United States is consequently given a very high status in South Sudan. One refugee in Bor explained that America is just one step below God. Whether or not one agrees with such adulation, it reflects the deep connection that exists for them between God and the world's political forces—all through the Lost Boys. In this understanding of God's saving acts, God is working not only through a group of young Sudanese men but through other (what they consider to be) Christian nations and the political process as well.

Even the Lost Boys' participation in the global economy is not beyond God's purview for the Dinka. As they choose their wives from Sudan and send money from the United States for the purchase of cattle, they serve to restore the marriage dowry system, thus bringing blessing to the community and stabilization to the local economy. The influx of money collected from dowries as well as remittances (money wired to family from refugees in the United States) is used for education, medicine, food, and the creation of businesses.[10] On some level, the Lost Boys are reconstructing the local economy in South Sudan.

Elders and important religious authorities continue to reinforce the role of the Lost Boys in the future of South Sudan. In the spring of 2009, I received word that "Uncle H.," a great leader and clan elder, died. In his last telephone conversation with my translator, a Lost Boy, Uncle H. charged him to "Remember that you are the seed of the community. God had a plan when He brought you to America so you could be our ambassadors. You must not forget your God or your community." So important are these young men to the future of the Dinka that a bishop from the Bor Diocese of the Sudanese Episcopal Church continues to visit the United States at regular intervals for the sole purpose of checking on the physical, spiritual, and educational well-being of the young men. He moves from city to city and stays with the young men to eat and pray with them and to learn about their lives. His task is to nurture and further the progress of this young remnant, who are ultimately the future of South Sudan. This mentoring has helped sustain the Lost Boys'

10. The town of Bor has many small shantylike structures that serve as restaurants. Other businesses include motorcycle repair, auto repair, and cell phones. There is a small market where vegetables and meat as well as other foods can be purchased. A large part of the customer base includes the personnel from numerous NGOs operating in the area.

connection to the larger Dinka community through which they draw strength and purpose that leads to resilience.

It bears mentioning that though the Lost Boys are hailed as agents of God, the young men find themselves negotiating two worlds. They undeniably comprehend the responsibility they have for the future of their people. They are seen as the chosen few and have been elevated to a place of very high esteem in Dinka society. On the other hand, in America, the majority of these young men live at the lowest socioeconomic level. The obligations they feel to send money to relatives often compromise their ability to better their own lives. Some may take on a second or third job instead of continuing their education because money for family is in such demand. It is entirely unhelpful that family members from Sudan call regularly asking for, even demanding, money. Both the burden and the blessing of being a Lost Boy are great.

Messy, Ragged Edges of Real Narratives

When we focus on resilience in communities such as the Dinka, who must negotiate the ongoing threat of continued trauma through violence and impoverishment, we risk romanticizing the messy edges of daily life. But as the Dinka community looks to their future story, they do so in the full reality of these everyday challenges. Such messiness should not tempt Western readers to dismiss the narrative altogether. Rather, let us ask how the faith narrative is evidence of a community well practiced in holding such contradictions while not giving themselves over to them. Even in a resilient community where so many have managed not to become disabled by trauma, there are those whose physical and emotional injuries are invasive. These are individuals among the Dinka who bear deep wounds that do indeed interfere with a productive and responsible life. For example, the evening I arrived in Bor, the elders from the Abang community greeted me. One elder, who arrived after the others, came forward moving brusquely and speaking a bit more loudly than was necessary. I immediately sensed that something was very different about him. My interpreter and another man gently stepped forward to intervene as the elder slapped me a bit too hardily on the shoulder in a gesture of welcome. They continued to move with him in order to monitor his actions. I later came to learn that during the war, a mortar had landed within inches of him, leading to what, based on the description of injuries and behavior, I surmised to be a traumatic brain injury (TBI).

After years of care that required attention from fellow soldiers, friends, and family, his health and overall functioning improved. Though he continued to have periods when he was psychologically unstable, he eventually went on to marry and have children. Then, six months before our meeting, he and his young son were attacked by cattle raiders from the Murle tribe as they walked near his village. In a hail of gunfire, the child was abducted, presumably to be sold into slavery. He has not yet been found. It is hard to say to what extent the wounds from these many traumatic experiences continue to complicate the effects of his TBI, but together they clearly impair his ability to function.

The wounds of war show themselves in striking ways and sometimes exceed the ability of the local community to respond. While I visiting Kakuma Refugee Camp, one aid worker told me of a twelve-year-old Dinka girl who had been kidnapped during the war, raped repeatedly by enemy soldiers, and left for dead. She survived and found her way back to her family. Her family became part of the less than 1 percent of refugees selected for resettlement, only to be rejected a short time later when mandatory testing revealed that the young girl was HIV positive. In 2003 many countries banned the admittance of any refugee who was HIV positive. The United States only just removed this ban in January 2010.[11] Not only did the family of this twelve-year-old rape victim lose all hope of leaving the war-torn region, but their rejection alone served to announce her HIV status to the larger community. One day, without her family's knowledge, the young girl simply walked off into the desert of Kenya. This act that led to her most certain demise was intended to secure her family's freedom. No twelve-year-old should ever have to make this kind of sacrifice for the survival of her family— but many do. The only remaining option for the community is to somehow hold both the tragedy and the possibility that came at such a great cost. In truth, the failure in this story sits squarely in the hands of the very same Western countries because of their discriminatory practices against refugees (the world's most vulnerable), whom the Dinka have come to see as God's agents.

---

11. The travel ban that restricted admittance of persons determined to be HIV positive was initiated in 1987 and signed into law by President Clinton in 1993. The law was repealed in 2008, but the ban was not lifted until January of 2010 under President Obama.

Some Lost Boys in the United States have not flourished but have become addicted to alcohol and other drugs, seriously compromising possibilities for their employment and education as well as their commitments to the home community in Sudan. One such young man is the son of a woman whom I first met in Kakuma and then again in Bor. Because the young man spends his paycheck on alcohol, he does not send money to help his mother build shelter or buy food and medicine. I sat next to her lean-to covered in blue plastic while she lamented both her son's terrible struggle and her own loss. "Because of the alcohol, he cannot even keep a roof over his own head and certainly cannot help build one over mine," she said sadly.

These examples, and others like them, reflect individual challenges to thrive, due to traumatic injury faced by some from the Dinka community. They reveal a rupture in the community that sometimes occurs because of violations in the moral obligation of care and at other times results from it. In either case, the larger community does its best to right itself by maintaining a posture of holding for those caught in the fracture. The identity of the Lost Girls, for example, was forfeited because the young girls were assimilated into family systems, largely a means of trying to keep them safe; a young girl with HIV tragically sacrificed herself but did so for the good of the larger family. Though a Lost Boy in the United States fell victim to alcoholism and can no longer take care of himself, a Dinka brother took him into his own home to feed and care for him. Families in the Bor community, likewise, share what they can to help his mother with food, shelter, and crops to plant. Individual woundedness does not negate the power of this community to provide a deep place of holding that sustains them through the joys and pains of daily life. The goal of living in a community with such a deep moral obligation of care is not to build a perfect community but to learn how to live in an imperfect one with integrity and grace.

'Where is the church in all of this?' is a question we often ask of our own culture. The answer is simple: the people are the church. Pastors are unpaid employees and live among the same daily struggles as do the rest of the community. There are no pastor's discretionary funds to assist the hungry and needy who come knocking at the church door. Often the pastor is as needy as the visitor. One Episcopal priest spoke to me of the widows with children who come to the church seeking food and shelter. He offers them a space in the compound to sleep but shares how often he must say, "Daughter, we will have to pray to God to bring us food because I have nothing."

As we can see, the Dinka faith narrative, no more than our own, is ripe with challenge and contradiction. One of the most difficult aspects of the Dinka narrative for Western readers concerns the role of Dinka women. On the one hand, as a cultural outsider, I want to be cautious in my critique of this narrative; but as part of the global community of faith, I also must acknowledge the exclusion of women from this narrative. I do so in full knowledge that imposing Western expectations is nothing short of a colonization of the Dinka faith narrative. I see no alternative; the questions are too important. For example, can any faith narrative that overlooks the role of women as primary participants in God's restorative actions be accepted as fully authentic or complete? The Abang community has focused primarily on young men as God's agents of salvation for Sudan, but we lament the absence of the Lost Girls in this narrative and the loss of opportunity associated with their exclusion. There is no doubt that this reflects an incomplete vision for the future among the Dinka and highlights for me the notion that faith narratives are far from idyllic, tidy stories. Rather, they are messy, difficult, and utterly steeped in our human imperfections. We can be sure that our own faith narratives will be no less so.

All Dinka women have a disproportionately difficult life in both the refugee camp and the village life of South Sudan. Like women in many other countries, Dinka women carry the greater burden in household chores and child rearing. In Sudan they can become victims of beatings by husbands, who have certain cultural authority to "discipline" wives. As happens everywhere else in the world, this abusive behavior is exacerbated by the use of alcohol, which is often brewed locally in the outer villages. Ghost marriage, the responsibility of a deceased man's male relatives to marry and bear children with his widow, often puts women in vulnerable and violent situations. A women's shelter was developed in Kakuma to serve women who feared for their own lives and those of their children for these very reasons. Yet, widows left without a husband's family to help with food and shelter are also left in dire straits. Even for women who live in loving, stable relationships, life is very hard. Though these circumstances were not prevalent in the Abang community, they did occur.

What we cannot yet see in this faith narrative are the ways that women's lives are already changing in South Sudan, even if only in small ways, and how Dinka culture is struggling to embrace it. The voices of women are slowly coming to the forefront. Women now hold important positions in nearly every level of government, and a new Department of Gender Equality seeks to advance the cause of women in rural areas. Even some of these rural communities are beginning to accept and promote the education of women through high school and beyond. In this culture that still practices the custom of bridewealth, educated women are literally valued more highly than those who are not educated. Much to the dismay of some older women, men are beginning to help with what have been long considered "women's chores." Such was the case when one of the local male cousins began to serve food to the women during a feast I attended for the return visit of a Lost Boy. However much we might like to see this as a sign of progress, change comes more slowly for the elder women in this village, by whom he was well chastised for his breech of public etiquette. Truly, these are imperfect measures of women's progress in South Sudan and reflect the challenges of a faith narrative that lives out the daily struggle of a community; nonetheless, it does show some, perhaps small, movement toward the enhancement of women's lives, their equality in society, and their potential inclusion in the story of God's redemption. Lest we rest too comfortably by comparing our own notions of inclusivity to those of the Dinka, I suggest that our Western faith narratives will be no less challenged, though in perhaps different ways. There is yet much room for all of us to make our faith narratives and communities more complete.

These are a few of the human frailties and systemic failures that highlight an imperfect and fragile community still struggling to survive and sometimes to grow. The good comes in fits and starts and seems profoundly inadequate given the whole picture of ugliness that surrounds the suffering. Yet any distortions of the ideal community do not nullify claims of God's redemptive work through this relatively small group of refugees called the Lost Boys or the larger Dinka community. Rather, they urge us to remember, as the Dinka do, that the redemptive vision is one in which God's faithfulness is constant even when the human response is less so.

7

Nurturing the Faith Narrative

As my plane took off from the refugee camp, I looked down at the small figures waving goodbye. I knew I would never be able to remember each face and name of those I met in Kakuma; yet, when asked will you remember me, my answer had been, yes, I will remember you. I did not have the right to take away the hope that comes from believing even one person in a sea of "forgottenness" knows of your suffering.

—Field notes from Kakuma Refugee Camp, Kenya

FAITH NARRATIVES OFFER A WAY OF DESCRIBING OUR SURE belief that we are remembered by God. They are not just about telling a story but about placing our story into the larger Christian narrative in which our suffering is incorporated into the suffering of Christ's own. Even more important, our redemption is framed by God's promise, for Christians as revealed in Jesus Christ, who is defined by his saving acts for all humankind. For the Dinka, this is a personal sacrifice—in which they are intimately remembered by God.

Being remembered by God and a community of those who know our story speaks to the fundamental desire of traumatized communities both to be known in our suffering and to believe that we can transcend that suffering through relationship with one another and God. Here we come full circle to the concept of pastoral care as remembering and remembering—the reconnecting of community torn by trauma and loss suggested in chapter 1.[1]

What can the Dinka faith narrative teach us about building a resilient community? In this final chapter, we will consider what the moral obligation of care might look like in our Western context. It is not realistic to expect that this obligation will be constructed in quite the same manner. But we should not overlook aspects that might serve to strengthen our own communities in times of crisis. Likewise, what characteristics of resilience might we be able to nurture within our communities that will help move us toward a hopeful future?

Moral Obligation of Care in the Western Context

The moral obligation of care that undergirds the Dinka faith narrative is nourished by a powerful kinship structure deeply set in cultural traditions very different from our own. Yet if the moral obligation of care is to be helpful for building resilience in the Western context, we will need to reconcile its unique characteristics to our own culture. The objective of this moral obligation of care in the Western context, as in the Dinka context, is to embrace a radical form of empathy and a deep spiritual accountability toward the other. It is for us, in many ways, a forgotten way of living with others that attempts not to destroy a sense of individual personhood but to understand its deeper fulfillment as part of the larger whole—the community of faith.[2]

Certainly we see glimpses of a strong, caring community when tragedy strikes, but it is a limited and fragile reality lasting only as long as the chaos ensues. Once official helping agencies begin to sort the chaos, we drift back to our cocoon of individualism, secure in the belief that professionals are at work meeting needs. On the one hand, this is appropriate. Communities should make room for skilled assistance needed to overcome traumatic events. But what the Dinka have shown us is that the strength of a community's obligation of care and the way they make sense of tragedy through their faith narrative can be a

1. Patton, *Pastoral Care*, 27.

2. Though not reflected in the Dinka narrative, the ultimate vision of this moral obligation of care, certainly in the Christian context but in other faiths as well, expands beyond any one community of faith to a broader understanding of obligation and care for our global community.

profound source of resilience that enhances other efforts of care. Even when there is an inadequate availability of resources, communities of faith can become their own resource of strength and resilience. So, how do we encourage and lead communities of faith to live with a daily commitment to the moral obligation of care? To help us envision this, we will return to the three practices of resilience that helped the Lost Boys survive the violence of war. Creating a relatively safe space, constructing a communal trauma narrative, and articulating justice, each weaving in and through the other, are interdependent characteristics that frame the moral obligation of care.

Creating a Relatively Safe Space

The image of the Lost Boys as children gathered in a circle of safety to fend off lions on their journey across Sudan is difficult to forget. I suggest that Western communities will see a moral obligation of care at work when we too create a *circle of trusting compassion that serves to hold fear and loss within our community of faith*. For the Lost Boys, "safe space" was not a literal bricks-and-mortar building but a profound trust in community, over the individual alone, to create safety out of any place. Certainly, it is a simple fact that a group of children standing together created the illusion of a larger threat, in the eyes of the approaching lion, than would have only one boy. But the task of the circle was to contain fear because it was fear that would lead to death. The sad reality is that sometimes the fear did win, and a child fled the group in an attempt to outrun the predator. In these cases, children died. But more often than not, by trusting that together they could hold the fear, they survived.

How do we build a community of trust that will hold fear and loss during difficult times? First, we must be willing to participate in compassionate hearing. Sadly, relatively few know what it is like to feel the abiding safety of a community of faith that has the willingness and courage to hold the most difficult stories and confessions. Traumatic realities are especially difficult to tolerate because they reflect both the human failure of compassion between perpetrators and victims, but also because they make us aware of our own vulnerabilities and moments of helplessness. When we cannot share the fear that lies at the heart of our stories, it can become global in scope and incapacitate even the strongest individual. It also lessens the capacity for resilience in the larger community.

Though it feels somewhat counterintuitive, creating a safe space in the Western context also requires that we avoid closing the circle. I recognize that this may be the point where the metaphor of children guarding against the attacking lion begins to fail us. Nevertheless, communities of faith must tend to the question of whether our circles are open and welcoming to those on the outside. Whom are we excluding? On the one hand, this is the question of inclusivity and difference with which so many communities of faith struggle, some openly, others more reluctantly. But, in situations of community trauma, it is also a matter of examining our tendency when under threat to create an absolute enemy of the ones we wish to blame for our pain and loss. The Christian narrative that provides the larger context for the moral obligation of care compels us to welcome all who wish a place in our communities and asks us to do the difficult work of resisting the creation of an "enemy" against which we can quickly rally.

Creating a Collective Trauma Narrative

The Dinka make a commitment of caring through the collective nature of the story they tell about traumatic events. When the trauma has targeted the entire community, such as with war and displacement, they seldom begin with a personal experience. Rather, as one Dinka man says, "only after telling the story of 'us' can I tell the story of 'me.' When we tell what happened to us, we don't want to exclude any who have suffered. I don't own the story because it happened to all of us." Stories of trauma such as rape that are not collective in nature but target an individual do begin with the personal but always move on to include the community. The injury to any one of its members is a matter of importance to the entire community. "What happens to one," the Dinka man says, "affects all of us." In the voice of the communal *we*, the community determines how best to care for the individual, names the injustice, and joins the victim in seeking retribution.

Western communities will see the moral obligation of care at work when we can *order our stories of trauma and loss to include the communal "we."* Such ordering challenges the inclination of any one person to carry the burden of trauma alone. Indeed, especially in cases of collective injury, it discourages individuals from believing they can take ownership of a story that belongs to all. While we may resist the idea of *owning* a traumatic story, communally or personally, it is only through laying claim to the suffering that resilience can thrive. Ordering the story to include the communal *we*, further, gives voice to the pain and suffering for those who cannot speak for themselves. The very young and very old, the cognitively challenged, the mentally ill, and those who through no impairment simply cannot speak are among those whose story finds voice in the communal *we*. None are forgotten.

Highlighting the communal telling of a collective trauma need not threaten conventional psychodynamic therapies that give precedence to individual experience. The communal voice does not ignore the personal one. It does, however, place personal suffering into a larger context and may help combat the tendency toward isolation that trauma often inflicts on its victims.

Depending upon the actual experiences of trauma and loss that affect us, the task of ordering our collective story in the United States will likely be challenged by which *we* we choose to embrace. In the years since the attacks of September 11, the national *we* has been fraught with political divisiveness and challenges to patriotism. From Hurricane Katrina we learned that the ethnic *we* is a powerful resource, but it is a narrative challenged by discrimination on the national, social, and faith-community levels. The community of faith is fraught with its own difficulties. Here, however, we can turn to the sacred stories of our tradition to encourage us toward a communal vision of *we* that embraces the compassion and solidarity in suffering that lead toward resilience.

Articulating Justice

The Dinka believe that naming justice holds a profound power and is a necessary part of caring for the other. One Dinka says, "When we were in the refugee camps, it took many of us together to try and solve the wrongs. Even if we could not get justice, our talking about it was a way of teaching why the action was wrong for the future." Western communities will see the moral obligation of care at work when we *claim a place of justice by naming how the community has been violated—even if it is beyond our power to repair it.* When we continue to give voice to what is just, we acknowledge that justice always has value, and no effort toward it is ever wasted. Some may argue that talk about justice is empty unless it brings about change. The Dinka, however, show us that naming justice is a powerful statement of resistance that boldly declares that no act of violence can render justice mute so long as even one is left to claim its place among those who suffer.

Claiming justice ushers God into the space of crime and victimization. It is the community of faith's task to wade through the anger, lament, and bewilderment often encountered as they ask why a just God would allow tragedy to befall God's beloved. Even when we think we have figured these things out, it is not surprising to experience the need to ask again in the throes of great pain and loss. The moral obligation of care helps contain the tensions that arise as we search for ways of holding multiple perspectives on what is just as well as subsequent judgments about how to repair the breech of justice that affects us. Like the communal trauma narrative, the communal voices speak for those who have no voice, but are also meant to teach and inspire others on how to tend to this difficult process. Even when communal efforts toward correcting an unjust wrong seem futile, claiming the place of justice holds fast to the hope for a future in which justice will be more completely fulfilled.

Learning from the Faith Narrative of the Lost Boys

We have seen how the Lost Boys and the Dinka community as a whole have found a sense of meaning out of their own suffering. They do this by locating their own community within the larger Christian narrative and by recognizing that God's faithful presence does not foreclose on their own responsibility to maintain the moral obligation of care that binds them together. Rather, God's active and healing power depends upon a communal understanding that each has the ability and responsibility to contribute in some way toward the good of the whole. As a result, this faith narrative is at the root of Dinka resilience and has helped them overcome what might have otherwise been debilitating effects of traumatic experiences.

Pastoral theologians and other religious leaders can learn much from the example set forth in this Dinka faith narrative about building a resilient community, especially in the face of difficult and dangerous times. Even before tragedy strikes, we can strengthen our own communities by helping them create a communal identity based on a moral obligation of care toward the other and on a faith narrative in which the community actively participates with God in bringing change and healing.

Reading the Subtext

To hear that the Dinka believe war is a punishment from God sets us off on a difficult beginning to understand how faith narratives can help us. It quickly brings to mind the horrendously offensive claims by Pat Robertson and others after the terrorist attacks on the World Trade Center and Pentagon or the earthquake in Haiti—that, in a similar vein, the destruction was punishment for various sins against God. At first glance, these views do seem similar, but there is a great difference between them. As outsiders listening in on another community's faith narrative, we come here to a significant point in understanding the pastoral role of reading its subtext, namely by asking the question: How do we honor the otherness of the community and their narrative by faithful listening that meets the community where they are?

The most important aspect of this narrative lies in the community's drive to ask where God is in this great tragedy of war and loss. They are participating in a relationship with God simply by pursuing the question. This seed of agency combined with the building of trust that comes in the communal quest begin the steps toward restoring a sense of hope in a meaningful world. Pastoral theology can help frame such questions of God and self in times of crisis, allowing the community to find its own answers while yet strengthening efforts to maintain connection with God.

Even so, we must recognize, as Andrew Lester suggests, that some future stories, and I would add faith narratives, are more functional than others;[3] and this raises further questions about how pastoral theology should respond. I propose two markers to help guide us in determining the healthfulness of faith narratives. First, the difference between Pat Robertson's claim and that of the Abang community is that the Dinka narrative emanates from within the community itself; it is not imposed by an outsider. This perspective reveals the Dinkas' intimate struggle to understand their own relationship with God. The emic nature of this

3. Lester, *Hope in Pastoral Care*, 78.

theology will no doubt be defined by a fluid boundary. In the case of the Dinka, colonialist or missionary influences most certainly have a deep, somewhat hidden impact on their theology. But it is, most immediately, their story as told by the people about their relationship with God.

Second, one must consider whether the narrative propagates destruction or human flourishing in the context of that community. (Whether it may prove equally helpful in its specificity to another community remains a secondary question.) A functional faith narrative will reveal explanatory models that move toward growth and recovery, not discord and alienation. With this in mind, whether or not we agree with the Dinkas' theology, we can discern a powerful drive to frame their experience within the larger Christian story, that is, to make some sense of where God is in their exile and suffering. In this context, pastoral theology can honor a community's faith narrative while acknowledging the incompleteness of all such narratives.

Resilient Characteristics

Constructing a positive faith narrative that fosters resilience in communities who are enduring sudden violence or other traumatic experiences is a pastoral-theological task. In this regard, certain characteristics of the Abang community's faith narrative can stretch across the cultural divide to help us. Pastoral caregivers can help communities learn to develop faith narratives that engage sacred stories in light of their experiences, whether they are tragic or joyful. Sacred stories will hold varying degrees of authority depending upon the community. The Abang community understands Scripture to serve a literal function. But even more interpretive views of biblical stories help us find ways that God is reflected in the human experience. Pastoral theologian Herbert Anderson observes that "the Bible is a literary resource for validating human experience today even when it is not regarded as divine authority. . . . Our stories and God's stories are inextricably linked together . . . And when we hear our own stories retold in relation to a larger and deeper narrative, our lives are transformed in the telling."[4] Sacred stories help us transform and transcend our own stories of tragedy and despair.

Communal faith narratives can help us build a sense of agency within individuals, tolerate ambiguity, and move all toward a sense of

4. Anderson, "The Bible and Pastoral Care," 202–3.

meaning in the face of traumatic experience. Such narratives are developed and reinforced through everyday encounters within the faith community, acts of social justice, and various forms of worship, ritual, and education that engage sacred stories.

Agency

The following selection is from my field notes taken while observing a worship service in Bor (quotations represent pastoral translations):

> The Sunday service included general announcements, the children's choir singing and dancing. A healing prayer was offered during which those seeking healing came forward. Here the pastor shouted "there is no doctor but God" and offered prayers along with a laying on of hands. He also called mothers forward for a blessing of the newborns. The pastor offered a blessing for the governor and encouragement to those whose loved ones had died. He said, "I will offer prayers but cannot do it alone— we must have the help of others to pray." (Scriptures read were Matthew 24 and Exodus.) The message: "God chooses leaders like God chose Moses. Will we be like those in the wilderness who complained about Moses by complaining about our leaders? Are we going to store away all of our resources, or are we going to produce something? Not just pastors but everyone works for God. God created jobs. God has a job for everyone no matter how young they are, even the smallest baby."[5]

Throughout this service, I was witnessing pastoral care being extended to the entire congregation. Faith, the greatest resource in this land of so much want, was being harnessed to instill power and agency for action among those who arguably have the least political or economic influence in the world. It is within their power, and their responsibility, to bring God into the space through prayer for healing, to care for the grieving, and even to plant the seeds of development through collaborative production—everyone has some contribution to make. When one has been rendered helpless by violence and loss, a sense of agency, no matter how small, brings the first glimpse of power to calm both psychic and social chaos.

Likewise, the role given the Lost Boys through the Dinka faith narrative, whether seen as blessing or burden, helped transform them from

5. From my field notes, Bor, Sudan.

mere victims of an atrocious war to living, breathing signs of hope for South Sudan. Research suggests that for many in this group, whatever effects of traumatic experience they suffered were mitigated by their connection to the community, the drive toward education instilled by their elders, and, most important, their faith in God.[6] Janice Goodman goes further to note the sense of empowerment with which the Lost Boys face their future. Instead of being mired in the "victim of trauma" mentality, she says, "their present interpretation of themselves . . . [is] as survivors and agents of their own future."[7]

It is not enough for pastoral caregivers to lead communities in asking, where is God in these tragic events? We also build resilience by staying actively mindful of another question, how do we understand our own participation in the unfolding of God's promise? Because of the ever changing flow of world events and our own lives, church communities and individuals must continually dance with this question. The Dinka show us that regardless of what tragic, destructive, or violent event may befall us, God's promise continues to work in and through us. We have an important role working with God to build (or rebuild) our futures. Living toward this is a fundamental aspect of spiritual resilience. Pastoral theologian Homer Ashby suggests that "the spiritual dimension of a sense of agency is found in the African American saying, 'God will make a way out of no-way' . . . Where there appears to be no possibility for change, God is a resource guaranteeing that change will come."[8] Though Ashby does not place the emphasis of agency on the choices we are given in our participation *with* God, as I am doing here, he agrees that our ability to make choices and act upon them is not just an opportunity but an obligation. He says, "Having the opportunity to make choices but failing to do so is squandering a gift given to us from God."[9]

Agency has a deep connection to hope. At some point, hope is a choice. We cannot make, give, or force hope. Ashby agrees when he says, "Hope emerges out of a sense that things can change and, more importantly, that there is something that one can do to bring about the

6. Goodman, "Coping and Trauma," 1187; Schweitzer et al., "Coping and Resilience," 285; Luster et al., "The Lost Boys," 208

7. Goodman, "Coping and Trauma," 1182.

8. Ashby, *Our Home*, 45.

9. Ibid., 142.

change."[10] I believe this to be the most fundamentally unfair aspect of hope. Those who need hope the most, and are least able to seek it themselves, are the ones responsible for choosing it. What we see in the Dinka story is the remarkable ability to find possibility even within grave limitedness, and the courage to act upon it even in the face of an uncertain outcome. The task of pastoral care in traumatized communities is to provoke a similar courage of faith that believes it is not our actions alone that bring change but ours in combination with God's divine purpose.

Tolerating Ambiguity

Life in the war zone, or any place of violence and trauma, is messy business, and we should expect nothing less from our faith narratives. We must engage the reality of uncertainty, contradiction, and imperfection in the life of our community and its stories—any faith narrative absent these warrants caution. Further, pastoral caregivers should, in a sense, be advocates for teaching communities to tolerate a certain degree of ambiguity that remains after reasonable questions have been answered. When we have reached the nub of the questions why or how and can dig no further, such tolerance helps us to resist the absolute enemies and quick solutions for which traumatic wounds yearn. Such enemies and solutions make uneasy companions to spiritual resilience and healing. If we do not make room for this ambiguity, it will be difficult for any community to embrace change or yield to flourishing. Instead, they may too easily become mired in anger, hatred, and revenge—unable to move forward toward a hope-filled future.

We have seen devastated communities struggle with this very issue too many times in the past decade with differing results. In describing the contentiousness of interpreting tragic loss in the Columbine community, pastoral theologian Larry Kent Graham tells us, "When a compassionate citizen erected fifteen crosses in Clement Park in honor of every person who died at Columbine, outrage from some members of the community forced the removal of the two crosses symbolizing the life of the shooters."[11] Meanwhile, the tragic shooting in a small Amish schoolhouse in Pennsylvania in 2006 resulted in a very different

10. Ibid., 44.

11. Graham, "Pastoral Theology," 10.

community reaction. After a gunman killed five young girls and critically wounded six others, the Amish community astounded the nation by offering prayers for the shooter and his family; some even attended his funeral. These are two very different reactions to grave tragedy. All communities facing such tragedy will have to confront intense feelings of anger, victimization, and fear—sometimes even compassion—toward perpetrators, all complicated by unimaginable grief.

Led by the gospel, the community of faith has a difficult job. On the one hand, it has a responsibility, as the Dinka have, to articulate justice, or, put another way, to name injustice as we encounter it, especially under conditions of violence and oppression. Yet the faith community also has a responsibility to resist claims that make absolute judgments about others who have harmed us, and a responsibility to likewise forgo judgments about the possibility, or not, of redemption for these perpetrators. For example, we are called to be a force against those human behaviors and social systems that cause physical, psychological, or spiritual harm. Yet knowing the all the factors that render a perpetrator culpable in traumatic events is not always so cut and dry. Pastoral theologian Jeanne Hoeft observes, "From a pastoral care perspective . . . it is not so easy . . . to find perpetrators who are not also victims or victims who are not also part of the problem. It is not so easy to decide who or what is responsible for any specific violent act or for the violence that permeates our culture."[12] The greater degree to which we can resist the fixed dichotomies of "us and them" or "good and evil," the greater the chance that when we are wounded we can keep the future open with possibility. Hoeft continues, "[practices of care] will need to be able to avoid constructing 'pure' victims and 'pure' perpetrators but remain committed to power analysis, social justice, and accountability."[13]

Tolerating ambiguity is somewhat counterintuitive. Certainty, we believe, makes us feel safe, secure, and ready to move forward. Meanwhile, willing oneself to stand in a place of uncertainty or unknowing taps directly into the reservoir of anxiety that reminds us how little we are really certain of in the first place. Traumatic experience magnifies this anxiety tenfold by turning whatever assumptions normally rule our world upside down. Yet it is ambiguity that makes room for

12. Hoeft, "Toward," 39.
13. Ibid., 51.

imagination and possibility, that is, the ability to imagine things as they might be. Pastoral caregivers who nurture community faith narratives that tolerate ambiguity invite the possibility of change and hope for the future. And, though it is a complicated matter indeed, such ambiguity is necessary for forgiveness to be possible.

Finally, ambiguity makes room for the mystery of the sacred. Pastoral theologian Kathleen Greider reminds us that "multiple meanings, apparent contradictions, and mystery contribute to human life much of its depth and value. From a theological point of view, ambiguity's richness of possibility and meaning leads us toward that which is Holy."[14] In the context of communal trauma, we can expect that the ambiguous corners of our faith narratives will come under fire. Trauma causes us to seek sure answers in precisely the places where none exist. The strength of the faith narrative will lie in its ability to withstand this challenge until its members can once again embrace mystery as a place where one can engage the God of possibility and hope.

Making Meaning

Larry Kent Graham notes the following as a resource for the pastoral caregiver, and I suggest it is a resource for all in the community: "the capacity to claim one's life from the ravages of catastrophic disaster is made possible by imaging a compassionate God who 'never fails nor forsakes' the world . . . The pastoral caregiver affirms that without such a divine reality the capacity to endure, heal, remember, grieve, protest, and realize new possibilities would be senseless and impossible."[15] It is the role of pastoral caregivers to help communities uncover faith narratives that reveal this God in times of tragedy whether they feel God actively present or deeply hidden. Faith narratives not only instill in us a sense of agency to overcome the helplessness brought on by trauma but, ultimately, can provide a frame of meaning for our own suffering and, in spite of this suffering, can invite us to participate in the ongoing promise of hope and redemption.

The faith narrative allows us to place our own tragedy in the larger frame of the Christian story. Only when we can see beyond the weighty edges of our own pain and suffering can a community begin to see

14. Greider, *Reckoning with Aggression*, 17.
15. Graham, "Pastoral Theology," 14.

possibility for the future. Finding purpose that transforms our suffering into something meaningful is a process enhanced by our ties to community. But it is important to note that purpose does not address the why of the event itself. In other words, purpose is not a precipitating factor but what a community, or individual, *discovers* as a result of a life-changing event over which no one has control.

Researchers working with a group of young refugees, including Lost Boys, observed: "believing that there was something important that God still intended for them to do, they gradually changed their focus from what they had lost to what they were alive to do."[16] We find meaning out of a traumatic event when we discover a purpose in life that helps us transcend the suffering caused by the event itself.

I have spoken little about healing in this book. If understood in the traditional manner, that is, as a state of cure, I often find its use in terms of emotional trauma to be little more than a grand gesture toward an idealistic end. In the context of refugee life, trauma and suffering are ongoing. When the war stops, displacement, impoverishment, and injury continue and are daily realities that prevent any sense of healing as cure from taking hold. Even in the context of trauma within our own communities, trauma seems to defy the neat boundaries of healing and wholeness.

In spite of my reluctance to embrace healing as cure, I nonetheless find certain aspects of it to be quite hopeful. I understand healing to be an ongoing and dynamic process that begins when we bring our suffering into the presence of God. Certainly there may also be physical and emotional components as well. The communal faith narrative, in particular, creates a space for our pain within the story of God's love and redemption. Herbert Anderson says, "Healing begins when the wounding memories of the past are reached and brought into the light without fear or when wounds are intimately connected with the suffering of God. To heal, then, does not primarily mean to take pain away, but to reveal that our pain is part of God's pain and our sorrows are part of the greater sorrow of God."[17] Anderson is speaking particularly about the power of ritual to facilitate this process of healing. Ritual is, indeed, an important way of reinforcing and expanding our under-

16. Luster, "The Lost Boys of Sudan: Coping," 207.
17. Anderson, "How Rituals Heal," 43.

standing of how God is working within a community's faith narrative. He goes on to say that among the many ways they bring about healing, "Rituals foster coherence of meaning in spite of inevitable mystery because the deepest truths of life and faith are hidden in God."[18] This is both the mystery and the presence that filled the small church I visited in Bor when the elderly and ill mixed together with mothers holding screaming newborns to move forward for a blessing. After years of war, violence, and poverty, through communal prayer and the laying on of hands, the power of God brought pain and new life together into a moment of possibility.

Summary

What are the faith narratives of church communities surrounding Columbine High School, and what do they tell us about how these communities have coped in the years since the shootings? How have faith narratives across the country helped Americans cope with the devastation of September 11? What about parishes in New Orleans after Hurricane Katrina? Or how about Haiti? In *Trauma and Grace*, Serene Jones describes the task of the larger church in the face of trauma in the following way:

> *The church is called, as it exists in this space of trauma, to engage in the crucial task of reordering the collective imagination of its people and to be wise and passionate in this task.* As people of faith, the church enables us to be storytellers, weavers, artists, poets, and visionaries who take the repetitive violence of 9/11 and reframe it in the context of the story of our faith. We are called to help write the scripts of the Christian imagination as it seeks to bring order to this disorder, and we must do so in a manner that seeks the flourishing of all people.[19]

Priming communities for resilience requires a pastoral theological lens framed by recognizing the context of the suffering, creating a moral obligation of care, and the building of a communal faith narrative. We must begin with an ethnographic understanding of a particular

18. Rituals, according to Anderson, also serve to: contain intense emotions, console deep hurts, connect communities of care, link intense emotions and words, and create a holding environment (Ibid., 46).

19. Jones, *Trauma and Grace*, 31 (italics original).

local church community.[20] What are its traditions, rituals, myths, and structures of leadership—particularly the unwritten ones? How do its members describe their moral obligation of care as a community, and where are the roots of this obligation evident? How do they articulate justice? In particular, how do they come together to stand against injustice, whether it is found on an individual or societal level? In times of great violence or tragedy, how does the community tell the story of their *collective* pain and loss while still honoring what may be individual aspects? How do they understand, as revealed explicitly and implicitly, their participation in God's action of bringing change to the world? Nurturing communities toward these markers as a regular practice strengthens community and individual resilience so that in times of tragedy they can more effectively withstand the onslaught and more deeply ground themselves in God's promise for a hopeful future.

On my last day in Sudan, I visited with the elders from the Abang community. I came to ask my final questions of these wise women and men. Tell me, I asked, about hope. And the elder said, "Our hope comes from God. He is the air that we breathe. He is the sand that we walk on. Without Him, we would not have made it, but through Him we will have a future." This statement reveals the power of the community and the faith narrative they build—to find hope and possibility in God, who acts in and through us even when our world has come undone.

---

20. For an excellent resource, see Moschella, *Ethnography as a Pastoral Practice.*

Bibliography

Action by Churches Together International (ACT International). "Appeal to ACT Members, Kakuma Refugee Camp." Kenya: Lutheran World Federation/Department of World Service, 1999.

Adolph, David, et al. *Ethno-Veterinary Knowledge of the Dinka and Nuer in Southern Sudan, a Study for the UNICEF Operation Lifeline Sudan/Southern Sector Livestock Programme*. Nairobi: UNICEF, 1996.

Anderson, Herbert. "The Bible in Pastoral Care." In *The Bible in Pastoral Practice: Readings in the Place and Function of Scripture in the Church*, edited by Paul Ballard and Stephen R. Holmes, 195–211. Using the Bible in Pastoral Practice Series. Grand Rapids: Eerdmans, 2006.

———. "How Rituals Heal." *Word & World* 30 (2010) 41–50.

Anderson, Siwan. "The Economics of Dowry and Bride Price." *Journal of Economic Perspectives* 21 (2007) 151–74.

Ashby, Homer, U., Jr. *Our Home Is over Jordon: A Black Pastoral Theology*. St. Louis: Chalice, 2003.

Augsburger, David W. *Pastoral Counseling across Cultures*. Philadelphia: Westminster, 1986.

Ballard, Paul, and Stephen R. Holmes, editors. *The Bible in Pastoral Practice: Readings on the Place and Function of Scripture in the Church*. The Bible in Pastoral Practice Series. Grand Rapids: Eerdmans, 2006.

Berhane-Selassie, Tsehai, and Simenish Berhane-Selassie. "An Evaluation of the Kakuma Refugee Assistance Project for the Lutheran World Federation Department for World Service Kenya/Sudan Programme." Nairobi: Lutheran World Federation, 2001.

Bixler, Mark. *The Lost Boys of Sudan: An American Story of the Refugee Experience*. Athens: University of Georgia Press, 2005.

Bohn, Carole R., editor. *Therapeutic Practice in a Cross-Cultural World: Theological, Psychological, and Ethical Issues*. JPCP Monograph 7. Decatur, GA: Journal of Pastoral Care Publications, 1995.

Cardoza, Thomas. "'These Unfortunate Children': Sons and Daughters of the Regiment in Revolutionary and Napoleonic France." In *Children and War: A Historical Anthology*, edited by James Marten, 205–15. New York: New York University Press, 2002.

Clinebell, Howard J. "Pastoral Caregivers Respond to the Shadowed Mystery of Collective Trauma, Grief, Anxiety, and Rage." International Pastoral Care Network for Social Responsibility. Online: http://www.ipcnsr-peace.org/IPCNSR/sept11m.htm/.

Coker, Margaret. "Tragedy in Chechnya: A Son's Wish to Play, a Mother's Wary Approval and a War Not of Their Making Have Consequences for a 14-Year-Old Chechen Caught in Russia's Push to Grozny." *The Atlanta-Journal Constitution*, February 6, 2000, C7.

Collins, Robert O. "The Nilotic Slave Trade: Past and Present." In *The Human Commodity: Perspectives on the Trans-Saharan Slave Trade*, edited by Elizabeth Savage, 140–61. London: Cass, 1992.

Cordner, Michael G., editor. *Pastoral Theology's & Pastoral Psychology's Contributions to Helping Heal a Violent World*. Surakarta: The International Pastoral Care Network for Social Responsibility, 1996.

Couture, Pamela D. *Child Poverty: Love, Justice, and Social Responsibility*. St. Louis: Chalice, 2007.

———. "Demystifying the War in the Democratic Republic of Congo." *Journal of Pastoral Theology* 17 (2007) 15–26.

Couture, Pamela D., and Emmanuel Lartey. "Pastoral Theology in International Perspective." *Journal of Pastoral Theology* 17 (2007) v–vi.

Courtois, Christine A. "Complex Trauma, Complex Reactions: Assessment and Treatment." *Psychotherapy: Theory, Research, Practice, Training* 41 (2004) 412–25.

Davidson, Paul R., and Kevin C. H. Parker. "Eye Movement Desensitization and Reprocessing (EMDR): A Meta-Analysis." *Journal of Consulting and Clinical Psychology* 69 (2001) 305–16.

Deng, Francis Mading. *The Dinka of the Sudan*. Prospect Heights, IL: Waveland, 1984.

———. *Tradition and Modernization: A Challenge for Law among the Dinka of the Sudan*. 2nd ed. New Haven: Yale University Press, 1987.

Department of Health and Human Services. Administration for Children and Families. "Office of Refugee Resettlement Annual Report to Congress." (2002). Online: http://www.acf.hhs.gov/programs/orr/data/02arc9.htm/.

———. Administration for Children and Families. "Table III-1: Employment Status of the Lost Boys by Sex: 2002 Survey." In "Office of Refugee Resettlement Annual Report to Congress—2002." Online: http://www.acf.hhs.gov/programs/orr/data/02arc9.htm#6%20accessed%20October%2014,%202010.

Derib, Alebel. "Group Care and Fostering of Sudanese Children in Pignudo and Kakuma Refugee Camps: The Experience of Save the Children Sweden from 1990 to 1997." Stockholm: Save the Children, 2001.

Everly, George S., Jr., and Jeffrey M. Lating, editors. *Psychotraumatology: Key Papers and Core Concepts in Post-Traumatic Stress*. The Plenum Series on Stress and Coping. New York: Plenum, 1995.

Farley, Edward. *Good and Evil: Interpreting a Human Condition*. Minneapolis: Fortress, 1990.

————. "Reflecting on Some Reflections: A Third-Order Essay." *Religious Studies Review* 24 (1998) 152–54.

Fickes, Michael L. "'They Could Not Endure That Yoke': The Captivity of Pequot Women and Children after the War of 1637." *The New England Quarterly* 73 (2000) 58–81.

First, Michael, editor. *Diagnostic and Statistical Manual of Mental Disorders.* 4th ed. Washington, DC: American Psychiatric Association, 1994.

Folke, Carl, et al. "Synthesis: Building Resilience and Adaptive Capacity in Social-Ecological systems." *In Navigating Social-Ecological Systems: Building Resilience for Complexity and Change,* edited by Fikret Burkes, et al., 352–87. Cambridge: Cambridge University Press, 2003.

Franks, Robert H. *Falling Behind: How Rising Inequality Harms the Middle Class.* The Aaron Wildavsky Forum for Public Policy 4. Berkeley: University of California Press, 2007.

Friedman, Matthew J. "PTSD Revisions Proposed for *DSM-5,* with Input from Array of Experts." *Psychiatric News* 45 (May 21, 2010) 8–33

Gamanga, Abu Bakr, and Virginia de la Guardia. "A Childhood Lost." Online: http://www.redcross.int/EN/mag/magazine2003_2/10-11.html/.

Geertz, Clifford. *The Interpretation of Cultures: Selected Essays.* New York: Basic Books, 1973.

Geltman, Paul L., et al. "The 'Lost Boys of Sudan': Functional and Behavioral Health of Unaccompanied Refugee Minors Resettled in the United States." *Archives of Pediatrics and Adolescent Medicine* 159 (2005) 585–91.

Gonsalves, Carlos J. "Psychological Stages of the Refugee Process: A Model for Therapeutic Interventions." *Professional Psychology: Research and Practice* 23 (1992) 382–89.

Goodman, Janice H. "Coping with Trauma and Hardship among Unaccompanied Refugee Youths from Sudan." *Qualitative Health Research* 14 (2004) 1177–96.

Graham, Larry Kent. "Pastoral Theology and Catastrophic Disaster." *Journal of Pastoral Theology* 16 (2006) 1–17.

Greider, Kathleen J. *Reckoning with Aggression: Theology, Violence, and Vitality.* Louisville: Westminster John Knox, 1997.

Harvard Program in Refugee Trauma. "Harvard Trauma Questionnaire (HTQ)." Online: http://www.hprt-cambridge.org/Layer3.asp?page_id=9.

————. "Hopkins Symptoms Checklist." No pages. Online: http://www.hprt-cambridge.org/layer3.asp?page_id=10.

Heptinstall, Ellen, et al. "PTSD and Depression in Refugee Children: Associations with Pre-Migration Trauma and Post-Migration Stress." *European Child & Adolescent Psychiatry* 13 (2004) 377–80.

Herman, Judith Lewis. "Complex PTSD: A Syndrome in Survivors of Prolonged and Repeated Trauma." In *Psychotraumatology: Key Papers and Core Concepts in Post-Traumatic Stress,* edited by George S. Everly, Jr., and Jeffrey M. Lating, 377–91. The Plenum Series on Stress and Coping. New York: Plenum, 1992.

————. *Trauma and Recovery: The Aftermath of Violence—From Domestic Abuse to Political Terror.* Rev. ed. New York: Basic Books, 1997.

Higgins, Gina O'Connell. *Resilient Adults: Overcoming a Cruel Past.* San Francisco: Jossey-Bass, 1994.

Hinton, Devon E., et al. "CBT for Vietnamese Refugees with Treatment-Resistant PTSD and Panic Attacks: A Pilot Study." *Journal of Traumatic Stress* 17 (2004) 429–33.

Hobfoll, Stevan E. *Stress, Culture, and Community: The Psychology and Philosophy of Stress.* The Plenum Series on Stress and Coping. New York: Plenum, 1998.

Hoeft, Jeanne. "Toward a Pastoral Theology of Resistance to Violence." *The Journal of Pastoral Theology* 16 (2006) 35–52.

Hodgson, Dorothy L. *Gendered Modernities: Ethnographic Perspectives.* New York: Palgrave, 2001.

Hollifield, Michael, et al. "Measuring Trauma and Health Status in Refugees: A Critical Review." *The Journal of the American Medical Association* 288 (2002) 611–21.

Holt, P. M., and M. W. Daly. *A History of the Sudan from the Coming of Islam to the Present Day.* 5th ed. Essex, UK: Longman, 2000.

Human Rights Watch. "New Video, New Photo Essay Tell Story of Uganda's Child 'Night Commuters.'" Online: http://www.hrw.org/en/news/2005/08/20/new-video-photo-essay-tell-story-uganda-s-child-night-commuters/.

Integrated Regional Information Networks (IRIN). "Kenya: Thousands of Refugees in Danger from Floodwater." Online: http://www.irinnews.org/Report.aspx?ReportId=45037.

———. "Kenya: Feature—Marginalised Turkana Vie with Refugees." Online: http://www.irinnews.org/Report.aspx?ReportId=45076.

Janoff-Bulman, Ronnie. *Shattered Assumptions: Towards a New Psychology of Trauma.* New York: Free Press, 1992.

Jones, Serene. *Trauma and Grace: Theology in a Ruptured World.* Louisville: Westminster John Knox, 2009.

Kalweit, Holger. *Shamans, Healers, and Medicine Men.* Translated by Michael H. Kohn. Boston: Shambhala, 1987.

Keen, David. *The Benefits of Famine: A Political Economy of Famine and Relief in Southwestern Sudan, 1983–1989.* Princeton: Princeton University Press, 1994.

Khalid, Mansour. *War and Peace in Sudan: A Tale of Two Countries.* London: Kegan Paul, 2003.

Kirmayer, Laurence J., and Allan Young. "Culture and Somatization: Clinical, Epidemiological, and Ethnographic Perspectives." *Psychosomatic Medicine* 60 (1998) 420–30.

Kleinman, Arthur. "Anthropology and Psychiatry: The Role of Culture in Cross-Cultural Research on Illness." *British Journal of Psychiatry* 151 (1987) 447–54.

———. *The Illness Narratives: Suffering, Healing, and the Human Condition.* New York: Basic Books, 1988.

Koenig, Harold G. *Faith and Mental Health: Religious Resources for Healing.* Philadelphia: Templeton Foundation Press, 2005.

LaMothe, Ryan. *Empire Matters: Implications for Pastoral Care.* Journal of Pastoral Care and Counseling 61. Supplement 5. Kutztown, PA: Journal of Pastoral Care Publications, 2007.

Landau, Judith, and Jack Saul. "Facilitating Family and Community Resilience in Response to Major Disaster." In *Living beyond Loss: Death in the Family,* edited by Froma Walsh and Monica McGoldrick, 285–309. 2nd ed. New York: Norton, 2004.

Lartey, Emmanuel Y. "Globalization, Internationalization, and Indigenization of Pastoral Care and Counseling." In *Pastoral Care and Counseling: Redefining the Paradigms*, edited by Nancy J. Ramsay, 87–108. Nashville: Abingdon, 2004.

———. *In Living Color: An Intercultural Approach to Pastoral Care and Counseling.* 2nd ed. London: Kingsley, 2003.

Lating, Jeffrey M., et al. "Psychological Assessment of PTSD." In *Psychotraumatology: Key Papers and Core Concepts in Post-Traumatic Stress*, edited by Donald Meichenbaum, 103–27. The Plenum Series on Stress and Coping. New York: Plenum, 1995.

Lawler, Edward J. "An Affect Theory of Social Exchange." *The American Journal of Sociology* 107 (2001) 321–54.

Lawrence, Mark, et al. "Household Food Economy Assessment in Kakuma Refugee Camp." United Kingdom: Save the Children Fund, 2001. Online: http://fex.en-nonline.net/1/household.aspx/.

Lester, Andrew D. *Hope in Pastoral Care and Counseling.* Louisville: Westminster John Knox, 1995.

Lienhardt, R. Godfrey. *Divinity and Experience: The Religion of the Dinka.* Oxford: Oxford University Press, 1961.

Luster, T., et al. "The Lost Boys of Sudan: Coping with Ambiguous Loss and Separation from Parents." *American Journal of Orthopsychiatry* 79 (2009) 203–11.

Lustig, Stuart L., et al, "Testimonial Psychotherapy for Adolescent Refugees: A Case Series." *Transcultural Psychiatry* 41 (2004) 31–45.

Lutheran World Federation/Department of World Service. *Annual Report of the Lutheran World Federation/Department of World Service Kenya/Sudan Programme.* Nairobi: Lutheran World Federation/Department of World Service, 2002.

Machel, Graça. *The Impact of War on Children: A Review of Progress since the 1996 United Nations Report on the Impact of Armed Conflict on Children.* London: Hurst, 2001.

Mbiti, John. "The Encounter of Christian Faith and African Religion." In *Third World Liberation Theologies: A Reader*, edited by Deane William Firm, 199–204. Maryknoll, NY: Orbis, 1986.

Miller-McLemore, Bonnie J. "Feminist Theory in Pastoral Theology." In *Feminist and Womanist Pastoral Theology*, edited by Bonnie J. Miller-McLemore and Brita L. Gill-Austern, 77–94. Nashville: Abingdon, 1999.

———. "The Living Human Web: Pastoral Theology at the Turn of the Century." In *Through the Eyes of Women: Insights for Pastoral Care*, edited by Jeanne Stevenson Moessner, 9–26. Minneapolis: Fortress, 1996.

———. "Pastoral Theology as Public Theology: Revolutions in the 'Fourth Area.'" In *Pastoral Care and Counseling: Redefining the Paradigms*, edited by Nancy J. Ramsay, 45–54. Nashville: Abingdon, 2004.

Mollica, Richard F., et al. "Science-Based Policy for Psychosocial Interventions in Refugee Camps: A Cambodian Example." *The Journal of Nervous and Mental Disease* 190 (2002) 58–66.

Moschella, Mary Clark. *Ethnography as a Pastoral Practice: An Introduction.* Cleveland: Pilgrim, 2008.

Nader, Kathleen, et al., editors. *Honoring Differences: Cultural Issues in the Treatment of Trauma and Loss.* The Series in Trauma and Loss. Philadelphia: Brunner/Mazel, 1999.

Neuner, Frank, et al. "A Comparison of Narrative Exposure Therapy, Supportive Counseling, and Psychoeducation for Treating Posttraumatic Stress Disorder in an African Refugee Settlement." *Journal of Consulting and Clinical Psychology* 72 (2004) 579–87.

Nhial, Abraham, and DiAnn Mills. *Lost Boy No More: A True Story of Survival and Salvation.* Nashville: Broadman & Holman, 2004.

Nsamenang, Bame A. "Early Childhood Care and Education in Cameroon." In *Child Care in Context: Cross-Cultural Perspectives*, edited by Michael E. Lamb, et al., 419–39. Hillsdale, NJ: Erlbaum, 1992.

Pargament, Kenneth I. *The Psychology of Religion and Coping: Theory, Research, Practice.* New York: Guilford, 1997.

Patton, John. *Pastoral Care in Context: An Introduction to Pastoral Care.* Louisville: Westminster John Knox, 1993.

Poling, James. "Creativity, Generativity, and the Next Generation." *The Journal of Pastoral Theology* 19 (2009) 94–103.

Ramsay, Nancy J. "A Time of Ferment and Redefinition." In *Pastoral Care and Counseling: Redefining the Paradigms*, edited by Nancy J. Ramsay, 1–43. Nashville: Abingdon, 2004.

Ressler, E. M., et al. *Children in War: A Guide to the Provision of Services.* New York: UNICEF, 1993.

Ripinsky-Naxon, Michael. *The Nature of Shamanism: Substance and Function of a Religious Metaphor.* Albany: SUNY Press, 1993.

Rittenhouse, Joan. "Using Eye Movement Desensitization and Reprocessing to Treat Complex PTSD in a Biracial Client." *Cultural Diversity and Ethnic Minority Psychology* 6 (2000) 399–408.

Savage, Elizabeth. *The Human Commodity: Perspectives on the Trans-Saharan Slave Trade.* London: Cass, 1992.

Save the Children Fund in the United Kingdom. "Save the Children Fund: Kenya Refugee Study Food Economy Updates of Kakuma Camps 1, 2, and 3, Kakuma Turkana District, Kenya." Nairobi: Save the Children Fund, 1999.

Scarry, Elaine. *The Body in Pain: The Making and Unmaking of the World.* New York: Oxford University Press, 1985.

Schweitzer, Robert, et al. "Coping and Resilience in Refugees from the Sudan: A Narrative Account." *Australian and New Zealand Journal of Psychiatry* 41 (2007) 282–88.

Summerfield, Derek. "A Critique of Seven Assumptions behind Psychological Trauma Programmes in War-Affected Areas." *Social Science & Medicine* 48 (1999) 1449–62.

———. "Effects of War: Moral Knowledge, Revenge, Reconciliation, and Medicalised Concepts of 'Recovery.'" *British Medical Journal* 325 (2004) 381–88.

———. "The Invention of Post-Traumatic Stress Disorder and the Social Usefullness of a Psychiatric Category." *British Medical Journal* 322 (2001) 95–98.

Starns, Penny Elaine, and Martin L. Parsons. "Against Their Will: The Use and Abuse of British Children during the Second World War." In *Children and War: A Historical Anthology,* edited by James Marten, 266–78. New York: New York University Press, 2002.

Sterling, Eric. "Rescue and Trauma: Jewish Children and the Kindertransports during the Holocaust." In *Children and War: A Historical Anthology,* edited by James Marten, 63–74. New York: New York University Press, 2002.

Teicher, Martin H. "Scars That Won't Heal: The Neurobiology of Child Abuse." *Scientific American*, March 2002, 68–75.

Thornton, Sharon G. *Broken yet Beloved: A Pastoral Theology of the Cross.* St. Louis: Chalice, 2002.

Tidball, Derek. "The Bible in Evangelical Spirituality." In *In The Bible in Pastoral Practice: Readings in the Place and Function of Scripture in the Church*, edited by Paul Ballard and Stephen R. Holmes, 258–74. Using the Bible in Pastoral Practice Series. Grand Rapids: Eerdmans, 2006.

Toledano, Ehud R. *The Ottoman Slave Trade and Its Suppression: 1840–1890.* Princeton Studies on the Near East. Princeton: Princeton University Press, 1982.

Tong, Benson. "Race, Culture, and Citizenship among Japanese American Children and Adolescents during the Internment Era." *Journal of American Ethnic History* (Spring 2004) 3–40.

Tutu, Desmond, with Douglas Abrams. *God Has a Dream: A Vision of Hope for Our Time.* New York: Doubleday, 2004.

United Nations Children's Fund (UNICEF). "The State of the World's Children 1996: Famine and Disease." Online: http://www.unicef.org/sowc96/5famdis.htm/.

United Nations Commission on Human Rights, Fifty-Second Session. "Addendum, Report of the Special Rapporteur on Violence against Women, Its Causes and Consequences, Ms. Radhika Coomaraswamy, Report on the Mission to the Democratic People's Republic of Korea, the Republic of Korea and Japan on the Issue of Military Sexual Slavery in Wartime, January 4, 1996." Online: http://www1.umn .edu/humanrts/commission/country52/53-add1.htm.

United Nations High Commissioner for Refugees. *Refugee Children and Adolescents,* 17 October 1997, No. 84 (XLVIII) 1997. Online: http://www.unhcr.org/refworld/ docid/3ae68c68c.html/.

United States Department of Health and Human Services. Administration to Children and Families. "Office of Refugee Resettlement Annual Report to Congress." 2002. Online: http://www.acf.hhs.gov/programs/orr/data/arc_02.htm/.

United States Senate. Committee on Governmental Affairs. Subcommittee on Oversight of Government Management, Restructuring. *Testimony of Jason Phillips, Country Director, International Rescue Committee, Kenya—Half a Loaf?—The Impact of Excluding Surplus Commodities from America's Response to Global Hunger.* 107th Cong., 2nd sess., 2002. Committee Print 80-603.

Walker, Williston, et al. *A History of the Christian Church.* 4th ed. New York: Scribner, 1985.

Walsh, Froma. *Strengthening Family Resilience.* 2nd ed. New York: Guildford. 2006.

Weine, Stevan M., et al. "Testimony Psychotherapy in Bosnian Refugees: A Pilot Study." *The American Journal of Psychiatry* 155 (1998) 1720–26.

Werner, Emmy E., and Ruth S. Smith. *Vulnerable, but Invincible: A Longitudinal Study of Resilient Children and Youth.* New York: Adams, Bannister, Cox, 1989.

Wessels, Michael. "Culture, Power, and Community: Intercultural Approaches to Psychosocial Assistance and Healing." In *Honoring Differences: Cultural Issues in the Treatment of Trauma and Loss*, edited by Kathleen Nader et al., 267–82. The Series in Trauma and Loss. Philadelphia: Brunner/Mazel, 1999.

Winnicott, D. W. *Playing and Reality.* New York: Basic Books, 1971.

Wood, Elizabeth J. "The Ethical Challenges of Field Research in Conflict Zones." *Qualitative Sociology* 29 (2006) 373–86.

Woodruff, A. W., et al. "Infants in Juba, Southern Sudan: The First Twelve Months of Life." *The Lancet* 324 (1984) 506–9.

Woolf, Henry Bosley, editor-in-chief. *Webster's New Collegiate Dictionary.* Springfield, MA: Merriam, 1981.

Young, Allan. *The Harmony of Illusions: Inventing Post-Traumatic Stress Disorder.* Princeton: Princeton University Press, 1995.

Zutt, Johannes. *Children of War: Wandering Alone in Southern Sudan.* New York: UNICEF, 1994.

Index